MW00332980

COLUMBUS

CHRONICLES

COLUMBUS

CHRONICLES

Tales from East Mississippi

RUFUS WARD

THE
History
PRESS

Published by The History Press
Charleston, SC 29403
www.historypress.net

Copyright © 2012 by Rufus Ward
All rights reserved

*Unless otherwise credited, photographs and images are from the author's collection or the Billups-Garth
Foundation collection.*

First published 2012

ISBN 9781540232755

Library of Congress CIP data applied for.

Notice: The information in this book is true and complete to the best of our knowledge. It is
offered without guarantee on the part of the author or The History Press. The author and
The History Press disclaim all liability in connection with the use of this book.

CONTENTS

CONTENTS

CONTENTS

ACKNOWLEDGEMENTS

For several years, Birney Imes, the editor/publisher of the *Columbus Commercial Dispatch* and an old friend, had discussed with me the idea of writing a weekly history column. Early in 2010, I decided that I would give it a try. The idea was to use the platform of the newspaper to explore the history of northeast Mississippi and west Alabama. We pondered different names for what would be a regular Sunday feature. As I was frequently asked questions about local history, we played with names such as "Ask Captain Possum." Around 1820, the Choctaws referred to Columbus as Possum's Town after an early storekeeper, Spirus Roach, who had a long pointed nose.

We finally settled on the less colorful "Ask Rufus," and my first column appeared in the *Dispatch* on February 27, 2010. I have since written over 125 stories of local and regional history for the paper and several other articles for magazines or journals. I have been amazed at the number of people who now stop me to ask questions about history and provide tidbits of information that they have heard or uncovered.

It has also been interesting to see how columns have been picked up by other publications and by people researching topics that I had written about. I have received inquiries concerning columns from people scattered from Los Angeles to London. A column I wrote about Memorial Day even resulted in my being interviewed for a *New York Times* article last spring.

People have often asked me about the source of my columns and how I learned so much little-known information. That answer is an easy one. I have some very knowledgeable close friends to call on. Depending on the topic, I am always calling them for help or suggestions, and they always respond. These columns would have been a real chore without the help of architect Sam Kaye, S.D. Lee Home, curator Carolyn Kaye, civil engineer Gary Lancaster, the Columbus-Lowndes Public Library, Billups-Garth Archives' archivist Mona Vance, State Archives and History Historic Preservation Division Director Ken P'Pool, historic archaeologist Jack Elliott and MUW Plymouth Bluff Center's Harry Sherman. My wife, Karen, has put up with scattered books and helps with suggestions while keeping me on track. Birney Imes has allowed me freedom to cover any topic that I have wanted to explore. In all, it has been a lot of fun to write the columns.

The articles that are in this book are those that seemed most popular or ones that I just found interesting. Some of my favorite stories, such as "The Crawford Panic," were a result of people who had read my columns calling or emailing me and asking, "Have you ever heard about this?"

Several friends and relatives who provided me with wonderful stories have passed away in the last few years. This has made me very cognizant of the need to preserve the stories of a passing generation. I hope that, with this book and my column, I can help do that.

Chapter 1

THE SETTLEMENT OF COLUMBUS

FORT SMITH, MISSISSIPPI TERRITORY, 1813–1814

Although not often mentioned, our area actually played an important role in the Creek Indian War phase of the War of 1812.

In 1813, with the eruption of hostilities with the Creek Indians, John Pitchlynn fortified his residence at Plymouth Bluff, and it became known as Fort Smith. Few people are aware of this historic site, which is only about four miles up the Tombigbee from present-day downtown Columbus, even though it is the only Mississippi site listed in the 2007 National Park Service "Report to Congress on the Historic Preservation of Revolutionary War and War of 1812 Sites in the United States" as a preservation priority site needing further study.

John Pitchlynn, Choctaw subagent and U.S. interpreter for the Choctaw Nation, established his residence at Plymouth Bluff at the mouth of Tibbee Creek in 1810 to help facilitate the movement of U.S. goods down the Tombigbee River. Although Columbus was established as a result of the construction of the military road that was surveyed in 1817, its foundation actually began with John Pitchlynn establishing his residence at Plymouth Bluff in 1810.

In 1810, Mobile was still under Spanish control, and the Spanish there were restricting the movement of U.S. military supplies along the Tombigbee. A new route for U.S. supplies had to be developed. Between

John Pitchlynn's fortified 1813 residence at Plymouth Bluff was known as Fort Smith. *Drawing by John Dunaway. Courtesy of Sam Kaye.*

1810 and 1814, four major shipments of U.S. goods that had originated in Pittsburgh passed down the Ohio and Tennessee Rivers, then by land to Pitchlynn's and again by river to the U.S. Choctaw Factor at St. Stephens on the lower Tombigbee.

Pitchlynn's was referred to in the Creek Indian War correspondence of Andrew Jackson, General John Coffee, Colonel John McKee and Choctaw Factor George Gaines as a U.S. supply depot, a meeting place for U.S. officers and Choctaw leaders and an assembly point for the marshalling of Choctaws and Chickasaws prior to their invasion of the Creek Nation in support of U.S. military operations. Peter Pitchlynn, later a governor of the Choctaw Nation, recalled two occasions when the fort was approached by war parties who withdrew upon finding it well defended. The fort consisted of a log blockhouse surrounded by a wooden palisade and contained at least one cannon. At the request of Andrew Jackson, there was a guard (either U.S. or Choctaw) stationed there at various times.

The fort was probably named after Captain George Smith of the Tennessee Militia who, in the fall of 1813, had accompanied Colonel McKee to Pitchlynn's. McKee credited Pitchlynn with securing a U.S.-Choctaw alliance against the Creeks in the fall of 1813. Among the notables to stop at Pitchlynn's for supplies was David Crockett in October 1814.

In a September 23, 1846 letter, Peter Pitchlynn recalled his childhood at his father's fort during the Creek War. Pitchlynn's letter, from the Peter P. Pitchlynn Collection at the University of Oklahoma Library, provides a poignant look at life on the Tombigbee frontier during the war years of 1813 and 1814.

None were more exposed than we were to the tommahawk & scalping knife of the Creek Indians [being] *then the farthest settlement towards the Creek nation who you know had espoused the cause of England—which brought them in conflict with the Choctaws as well as the people of the United States. Twice had they come to attact us, but finding we were Forted and probably from a belief we were very strong in numbers they retired without making an attact upon us. I recollect how often we were alarmed by news reaching us that signs of the enemy were about us—One time Mother fled with us/the children to Yakmittubbe's about ten miles off. The alarm was great, brother James came up in full speed (father was not at home) with news that he had heard the war hoop of the Creek Indians—brother Joseph remained in the fort, being some four years older than myself—he said that if he was not able to fight he could run bullits for those that could fight—Mother cryed when she left him, but not without incouraging him to be brave—upon which Joseph painted his face and said he would die defending the Fort...The past how they crowd upon my mind, and how vivid are the recollections of my youth. I can without the least mental effort see the old homestead as she appeared during the war,—and the war fires blazing on her hills. The war dance, the war talks and many a brave and na humma, long dead now rise up in my mind—What brave noble fellows they were. They had come to the protection of my father, and family, and they would have fallen & died around our little fort ere they would have allowed a Muskoke reaching us with their Tomma hawks. Among those who figured in those scenes how few are living.*

The last military activity at the fort occurred in early 1815 when Pitchlynn fired the fort's cannon to celebrate the end of the war. The cannon exploded and Pitchlynn then commented, "Well we have no further use for her—she has served us through the war, and busted in telling us the news of peace." Pitchlynn's became a post office in 1819, but it was moved to Columbus in 1820. The town of Plymouth was established there in 1832, but by the mid-1850s it was all but abandoned. Today its site is on the west bank of the Stennis (Columbus) Lock and Dam. The Mississippi University for Women

(MUW) Plymouth Bluff Center, which contains excellent cultural and natural history exhibits, is located just south of the fort site.

THE ST. STEPHENS TRACE

The St. Stephens Trace is a little-known but very historic road that once ran from John Pitchlynn's residence at the present site of the John Stennis (Columbus) Lock and Dam to St. Stephens, which is about fifty miles north of Mobile. It evolved out of an existing Indian trail and was the first important north–south road in what is now east Mississippi and west Alabama.

The road ran south from Pitchlynn's to the vicinity of the intersection of Highways 82 and 45. From there it ran south to St. Stephens, roughly following the present route of Highway 45. When Andrew Jackson's Military Road was surveyed in 1817, it incorporated the St. Stephens Trace from just west of Columbus to near present-day Meridian.

The St. Stephens Trace played a major role in an old Columbus legend. The story holds that Andrew Jackson marched down Military Road through Columbus on his way to the Battle of New Orleans. This was a significant accomplishment given that Military Road was not even surveyed until 1817. What did transpire was that in October 1814, General John Coffee led three thousand Tennessee Militia south to reinforce Jackson prior to the fighting at New Orleans.

Coffee's route took him down the Natchez Trace to the Chickasaw villages (Tupelo) and from there down Gaines Old Trace to Pitchlynn's. On October 14, 1814, Coffee wrote General Jackson from Pitchlynn's that he expected to find better roads from "Peachland's" to Fort Stoddard than he had found from Tennessee to "Peachland's." The better road he referred to was the St. Stephens Trace. Out of that incident arose the Columbus Andrew Jackson tradition.

One of the most interesting historical documents is an old account of travel in the local area. There exists a 206-year-old account of traveling on the trail that became the St. Stephens Trace. In 1806 George Gaines traveled that trail, and in 1848, Albert Picket recorded Gaines's account of that journey.

The route of St. Stephens Trace crossed Magowah Creek south of Columbus, about a mile east of Highway 45. The old roadbed in Magowah Bottom is now covered by catfish ponds. *Courtesy of Aaron Hoffman.*

In going from St. Stephens to Colbert's Ferry in 1805 the trail led by the north west corner of Washington County [Alabama], *thence by the house of a Frenchman named Charles* [Juzan] *near the Lauderdale Springs— He had an Indian family having married a niece of Pushmatahaw— lived well in a neat cabin entertained travelers & sold goods to the Indians, was well respected by whites and Indians—was of a respectable* [French] *family—The Indian town of Coonaha was where he lived— This was the residence of Pushmatahaw also—The route through the old Yazoo towns to the Noxibee River & crosses near where the town of Macon now is where resided an Indian countryman, named Stores* [Starnes], *a sensible Yankee blacksmith, who had been living here many years with an Indian family & entertained travelers Half way between Stores & Pitchlynn's lived Muchilletubia* [Mushulatubbee], *who was the son of Hooma Stubbee, the Senior chief of the nation—Hooma Stubbee died indebted to the Factory* [the U.S. Choctaw trading establishment] *$1,000 in 1809 & his son assumed & paid the debt. Thence to Pitchlynn's, U.S. interpreter* [for the Choctaw Nation], *who lived near the mouth of Okatibbee* [Tibbee] *River.*

Driving down Highway 45, especially between Columbus and Meridian, takes on a new meaning when thinking of what that route was like two hundred years ago when it was known as the St. Stephens Trace.

THE FIRST BUILDING ON THE SITE OF COLUMBUS

The first structure built within the limits of the original town of Columbus was a log cabin built by Thomas Thomas in the fall of 1817. It was constructed on what is now Third Street South on the bluff overlooking Harvey's Restaurant.

The best early account of the cabin was written by Oscar Keeler in 1848: "In the latter part of the year 1817, Thomas Thomas, a man who had been driven out by the agent, as an intruder in the Chickasaw nation, built a small split log hut upon the ground now known as the residence of C.D. Warren, Esq...but there was no signs of it ever being occupied by any person till 1819."

Interestingly, Spirus Roach, whose "peculiarities" and features led to the Indians calling Columbus "Opossum Town," kept "entertainment" in the cabin in 1819.

By 1820, William Cocke and his family had built houses along what is now Third Street South between Main and College. The Cocke family had claimed that area where Thomas Thomas had first built a cabin. This raises a question about the relationship between Cocke and Thomas. Sam Kaye and I have often discussed this and wondered if Columbus was founded as a land speculation scheme. What we have found presents an interesting picture.

In the years following the Creek Indian War, the subsequent Creek Indian Treaty of 1814 and the Chickasaw, Choctaw and Creek Treaties of 1816, land speculation fever seized the newly opened Indian lands. In 1816, William Hawkins, son of longtime creek agent Benjamin Hawkins, wrote to the surveyor general of the Mississippi Territory inquiring about the best land in the newly purchased Indian territory, which he called "Jackson's purchase." With help from Andrew Jackson, John Overton and James Winchester claimed the land that would become Memphis in 1819.

So, where do Thomas and Cocke come into this?

In September 1814, William Cocke was appointed Chickasaw Indian agent and was expressly directed to remove intruders from the Chickasaw

Thomas Thomas's 1817 cabin at the site that would become Columbus. *Drawn for the author by H. Frank Swords.*

Nation along the Tennessee River. However, Cocke angered the Chickasaws by allowing some intruders to stay. The Chickasaws believed that such favoritism resulted from Cocke being married to Kissiah Simms (the sister of an intruder) and his close friendship with other intruders.

In September 1817, Cocke and Andrew Jackson were corresponding with each other regarding agency business. On September 30, 1817, Captain Hugh Young wrote to Jackson informing him of the location of the Military Road's Tombigbee crossing. That was information to which Cocke would have had access. In November 1817, Cocke was notified that Henry Sherburne would replace him as Chickasaw agent. In the fall of 1817, Cocke "drove" Thomas Thomas out of the Chickasaw Nation as an "intruder," and Thomas just happened to build a cabin at the Military Road's Tombigbee crossing. Cocke left the Chickasaw Agency in June 1818. By the following year Cocke and his family were living in the new town of Columbus on the site where Thomas Thomas had first built a cabin.

Did Cocke, as Columbus histories state, run Thomas Thomas out of the Chickasaw Nation? Or was he sent by Cocke to claim some prime land of which Cocke had received inside information?

AFRICAN AMERICANS AND THE SETTLEMENT OF THE UPPER TOMBIGBEE VALLEY

When the topic of antebellum black history comes up, most people immediately think of the horrors of slavery. While those horrors cannot be diminished, there is a whole world of black history that needs to be brought to the forefront. That is the roles of blacks—both free and slave—in the settlement and development of the Tombigbee River Valley.

The influence of blacks in the Tombigbee Valley began with the earliest European exploration. When the De Soto expedition passed through this area in the early 1540s, there were seven or eight free blacks serving with him. The French military forces operating along the Tombigbee out of Mobile in 1736 included a company of black soldiers under the command of Simon, a free black French officer. During the American Revolution, free blacks served in American and Spanish forces fighting the British in the Mobile area. The first man wounded in the 1780 Spanish-American assault on Fort Charlotte in Mobile was a free black man. Lorenzo Montero, another free black, commanded a cannon in a Spanish battery during the assault against the British. Unfortunately, the names of many of the blacks who played important roles in our earliest history have been lost.

After American independence, the role of African Americans continued to expand. The names of several of those pathfinders have been preserved. The earliest court records in Monroe County denote the activities of William Cooper, a free black man who was trading along the Tombigbee River as early as 1790. Cooper was both a horse trader and a contractor. In the early 1790s he was selling horses for fifteen dollars a head. He even traded a horse to acquire a slave by the name of Medlang, with whom he had fallen in love. She was a servant of John Turnbull of Natchez/Baton Rouge. At that time horse racing was a popular sport, and Cooper traded his horse Cooper's Grey to Turnbull for his bride. In 1794 Cooper was hired to build a fort on the Tombigbee, probably at St. Stephens, which is north of Mobile.

In 1842, African American engineer Horace King constructed a 420-foot-long wooden covered bridge across the Tombigbee at Columbus. *Drawing courtesy of Sam Kaye.*

In 1808, a free African American by the name of Betsey Lewis was living with her family in the lower Tombigbee area. It might have been at her house that U.S. Choctaw Factor George Gaines stayed while traveling in 1810. He recorded that on November 5 he "paid negro woman on 1st evening of journey for food, corn and fodder, 2.50."

In March 1814, Gaines transported supplies by flatboat from John Pitchlynn's at Plymouth Bluff to St. Stephens and had a crew of five including Dick, an African American. Earlier, in January 1814, Gaines had sent a factory (trading post) boat upriver from St. Stephens to Pitchlynn's at "the mouth of Tibbee" and then returned to St. Stephens. Two unnamed African Americans were hired to row the boat. Their supplies for the trip were listed as "1 gallon whiskey, 50 lbs of bacon, 2 bushel potatoes, venison, jerky, 3 dozen eggs, 1 bushel peas."

Between 1806 and 1816, twenty-two different African Americans were employed at various times by the U.S. Choctaw factory on the lower Tombigbee River. Unfortunately, only first names are provided in the records, and slave and free are listed together.

Free African Americans had an early impact on the history of Columbus. In 1822 there was a lumber dealer in Columbus by the name of James

Scott who was providing materials for the construction of houses in the new town. County records indicate that there were no whites in his household, thereby implying that he was African American. By 1843 Isaac and Thomas Williams were living in Columbus with their families. Both were African American. Isaac was a laborer and probably a contractor, and Thomas was a blacksmith.

The first major construction project in Columbus was the building of a bridge across the Tombigbee River. The bridge was built by Horace King, an African American engineer who, in the mid-1800s, was considered the best bridge builder in the South. He earned that reputation while a slave, though he later purchased his freedom and entered into partnership with his former owner. King built the Columbus Tombigbee Bridge in 1842. It was a wooden covered bridge that came off of the river bluff at Fourth Avenue South and was 420 feet long and 65 feet high. He also built bridges over the Luxapalila and Yellow Creeks, and those two bridges survived into the twentieth century. A 1936 *Commercial Appeal* article said the Luxapalila Bridge was ninety-four years old and was the oldest bridge in Mississippi.

The history of Columbus is filled with African Americans who played key (but often forgotten) roles in the town's settlement and development.

WHERE DID MILITARY ROAD GET ITS NAME?

Whenever something gets torn up, people tend to pay more attention. So it is with Military Road in Columbus. The street seems to be constantly torn up with the city working on improvements. That has resulted in my often being asked why it is called Military Road and if Andrew Jackson really marched down it on the way to the Battle of New Orleans in 1815. Military Road does have its origins with Andrew Jackson and the Battle of New Orleans; however, Jackson never traveled on it, and its route was not even surveyed until 1817. The road was built in response to the lack of a direct route from Nashville to New Orleans. Jackson realized that problem as he was attempting to marshal his forces in late 1814 prior to the battle at New Orleans.

In order to address the need for a connecting road, Congress, on April 27, 1816, directed that a survey for a road from Nashville to New Orleans be made. On September 30, 1817, Captain Hugh Young reported to Andrew Jackson on a proposed crossing point on the Tombigbee River.

The Military Road in Columbus circa 1905.

That location became the town of Columbus and was settled soon after the completion of the survey. The road was constructed by the First and Eighth Infantry Regiments and a detachment of artillery. In 1819, there was a work camp located on Howard's Creek about six miles northeast of Columbus. Two soldiers died there and became the basis of Joseph Cobb's "The Legend of Black Creek," an 1851 tale in the vein of Washington Irving's headless horseman.

The road to the Tombigbee and the new settlement of Columbus were completed by the spring of 1820. *Niles' Weekly Register*, a Baltimore newspaper, reported that the new road shortened the distance from Nashville to New Orleans by three hundred miles. In an article datelined Florence, Alabama, August 29, 1820, the newspaper stated, "The Military Road is now open from this place to New Orleans, and is probably one of the finest roads in the union. It has been opened under the immediate direction of Gen. Jackson."

Though Andrew Jackson did not march down the Military Road on his way to fight the British at New Orleans, he did have the road constructed to address problems in the movement of troops that occurred prior to the Battle of New Orleans.

The Oldest Surviving Houses in Columbus

I am often asked: "What is the oldest house in the Columbus area?" That is an easy question, for it is the Cedars, the oldest part of which was probably built around 1818. Tradition and physical evidence both indicate that the Cedars is the oldest house in Columbus and probably northern Mississippi. The Cedars sits on top of a hill overlooking the Military Road, which was surveyed in 1817 and was the first road through Columbus. Halfway between the house and the road is a natural spring, making this a prime building location. The earliest recorded owner of the property was Vardy McBee. The McBee family moved to present-day Lowndes County in 1817. There is no record, though, as to when he acquired the property or if he built the house.

People then often follow up with the more specific question of "What about the oldest frame or brick house or commercial or governmental building?" So what are the area's oldest buildings?

The first actual towns (as we know them) in the northern half of Mississippi were Columbus, Hamilton and Cotton Gin Port (which was located on the Tombigbee near present-day Amory). They were all located in what was, in 1819, thought to be Marion County, Alabama. Cotton Gin Port and the Henry Greer House (the site of which is now the Columbus Air Force Base) served for a time as the county seat of Marion County. By December 1819, the town of Columbus was a Marion County, Alabama voting precinct. It was in January 1821 that the Cotton Gin Port–Columbus area was declared to be in Mississippi and not Alabama. In February 1821, Monroe County, Mississippi, was established, and Columbus was incorporated as a Mississippi town.

Structures from those formative years are nearly all gone. Only two come to mind—the Cedars and Belmont, which was built in 1822, northeast of Columbus on Wolf Road (which got its name because of the many wolves that attacked livestock in the area). The original part of the Cedars is a single-pen log cabin, while Belmont may be the oldest surviving frame building in north Mississippi.

In 1830, Monroe County was divided, with the north half remaining Monroe and the south half becoming Lowndes. Columbus became the county seat for Lowndes, and Athens (south of Amory) became the county seat of Monroe. The old courthouse/jail remains at Athens and is the area's oldest surviving governmental building. The brick building that is now Back Door Columbus was built around 1830 and is probably the oldest surviving commercial building in Columbus.

The Cedars, originally built as a single-pen log house circa 1818, is probably the oldest surviving house in north Mississippi. *Drawn for the author by H. Frank Swords.*

Few of the buildings of Columbus's first decade have survived. Within the twenty-one blocks of the original town limits of Columbus, the Ole Homestead (circa 1827) is probably the oldest surviving structure. It may also be the third-oldest remaining vernacular raised cottage in the state. It was originally a two-room over two-room raised cottage facing the Tombigbee River. The McCartney-Hunt house was built around 1824 just outside the town limits on present-day Seventh Street. It is probably the oldest surviving brick house in north Mississippi and is of the Quaker or Swedish floor plan.

Within present-day Columbus (but outside of the original town limits) are several surviving log houses. The Cedars was mentioned earlier. Hickory Sticks on Seventh Street is a double-pen log house built during the 1820s and enlarged around 1834. The Moody House on the South Side was a log dogtrot built in the 1820s and later enlarged. It may have been moved from another location. There are probably a few other log structures buried inside of later houses. Magnolia Hill is an early raised cottage overlooking Military Road on the North Side and was constructed about 1832. On the South Side, Corner Cottage is a circa 1830 house that was originally just two rooms.

The original floor plans of the Ole Homestead and Corner Cottage, along with construction details of Franklin Academy in 1821 and Dr. B.C. Barry's house in 1825, show what may be the typical 1820s frame house in Columbus. That would be a two-room house that was thirty-five to forty feet wide and fifteen to twenty feet deep. While people often think of the early houses in Columbus being log cabins, after 1821 many were actually wood frame and several were even brick. In 1830 the town required that new buildings must be built of frame or brick, thus ending the construction of log cabins that are so associated with the frontier.

COLUMBUS IN 1822

People often ask me: "What did Columbus look like when it was first settled?" Thanks to Reverend George Shaeffer, that may be the easiest question to answer. In 1872 Shaeffer published an account of early Columbus titled *Columbus in 1822 by Its Oldest Inhabitant*. The description was republished in 1909 in Lipscomb's *History of Columbus*.

Shaeffer took his readers on a visual stroll down both sides of Main Street in 1822. It is a priceless description of early Columbus:

> *As may be supposed, Columbus was a small place when my eyes first beheld it in 1822. It contained about 150 inhabitants. Main Street presented quite a different appearance from at present; only a few scattering houses. On the south side at the west end, there was a large house composed of four rooms in each story, with a cross passage through the center each direction; this stood on the point of the hill. It was occupied by the venerable Judge Cocke, who called it "the big pile of logs." The next house, going east, was a one storied store about 20 by 30, a frame, kept by Judge Haden; it stood about opposite the postoffice. The next was a small two story frame store on the corner opposite the hotel, occupied by John B. Raser. Between that and the corner of Main and Market Streets, there was quite a hollow; the first house from Raser's was a log blacksmith shop in the hollow about half way the square. The next house was a small tailor shop. The next was a one story frame, standing sidewise to the street, about 50 feet long, occupied*

Barry's Tavern circa 1822. *Drawn for the author by H. Frank Swords.*

by Capt. C. Adams as a store...The next house was an old carpenter's shop on the Gross corner. There was a carpenter's shop on the corner occupied by Humphries and Hudson; from thence east and south was covered with pines and small bushes.

On the north side of Main Street, west end, there was a one story store kept by Capt. Kewen. The next building was a small retail whiskey shop; the next Barry's tavern, a two story house of pretty large dimension, a frame, but unfinished; it stood on the corner where the Gilmer hotel is kept. On the opposite corner (old Varsity Theater location)...stood a small two story framed house occupied below as Dr. Barry's shop and above as a Masonic lodge. From these, going east was no building, until after crossing quite a deep hollow, you arrived at a long one story house, occupied in part by Major William Dowsing as a tavern, and in the west end as a small retail store; this house was on Blair's corner (BanCorp South building today). Market street was not built upon. The balance of the village was composed of a few small log cabins scattered among the bushes. The Franklin Academy was a small frame house 30 by 40, not ceiled nor plastered; this was the preaching place for all denominations; the Methodist was the only organized church at that time, composed of a very few members.

Chapter 2

FIELD AND FOREST

JACK KAYE'S WINDOW TO A LOST WORLD

The recent passing of Dr. Jack Kaye has brought many memories of huge, strange creatures that once walked the Black Prairie. Dr. Kaye was the authority on the ancient life of the prairie and especially that of the Pleistocene epoch, or Ice Age.

He also developed a theory that an ancient Tennessee River once flowed down what is now the western flank of the Tombigbee River Valley. That theory explained the presence of gravel from the Appalachian Mountains along the route of the Tombigbee River.

It was through the Ice Age animals of the Black Prairie that Jack provided a new look at a lost world. Prior to his research there were only 321 Pleistocene fossils from Mississippi mentioned in scientific literature. Of those fossils, 80 percent were found around Natchez, and only five such fossils were reported from northeast Mississippi.

The Black Prairie had not been known as an important area for the finding of Pleistocene fossils until Jack found and identified thousands of them. Prior to Jack's work, only about a dozen Pleistocene vertebrate species had been documented in Mississippi. Jack's work produced a species list for the Black Prairie alone that amounted to more than forty Pleistocene vertebrate species.

His dissertation on vertebrate fossils of the Black Belt showed an almost unbelievable variety of animals living here from ten thousand to

The Ice Age landscape of the Black Prairie. *Painting by Amaria Smith Robinson. Courtesy of MUW Plymouth Bluff Center.*

forty thousand years ago. As strange as it seems, the prairie was once the home to zebras, camels, mastodons, mammoths, elk, giant ground sloths and giant beavers. In an area where few important mammal fossils had been found, Jack collected countless fossil examples, thereby opening a window to a prehistoric world. His scientific research, however, was not without its lighter moments.

Jack told of one occasion when he was exploring a creek bed and began finding scattered fossil bones of a mastodon. He started following the scattered fossils back up the creek to try and discover the location from which they had been washing out. After walking a good distance and crossing under the remains of an old fence, he encountered an irate farmer who wanted to know what Jack was doing trespassing on his land.

Thinking that the farmer might not know what a mastodon (a close cousin of the elephant) was, Jack replied that he had been for some distance following the tracks of an elephant and if the farmer didn't mind, he would like to keep looking, as it might be just around the next bend of the creek.

The farmer gave him a funny look and asked, "Tracking an elephant? Just around the next bend of the creek?" Then, as Kaye confirmed, the farmer turned to quickly get away and said, "Mister, don't mind me, you just look for all the elephants you want to."

Jack once found the complete mandible of a giant mastodon in a creek near Tupelo. He placed part of the huge jaw in a fossil display at MUW's Plymouth Bluff Center.

At Plymouth Buff, extensive beds of Cretaceous (seventy-five-million-year-old) fossils were once exposed. It was a favorite fossil-collecting location for many Columbus residents. The fossil remains of mosasaurs (huge seagoing reptiles), sharks and ammonites (related to the chambered nautilus) were often found there, and Jack was always ready to take the time to identify the fossils and give a natural history lesson to anyone who came to see him.

When I was growing up, Jack encouraged my interest in history and would take me fossil collecting. He also taught me the importance of research and recording the location at which artifacts or fossils were found. Mostly though he instilled in me a desire to learn and brought to life the prehistoric life of the Black Prairie.

"Lions and Tygers and Bears"

First during deer season and now during turkey season, radio talk shows and hunters have been discussing black panthers and their possible existence in Mississippi. Naturalists all agree that the black panther is not to be found in

An 1833 engraving of the Jaguar, which was "sometimes called the American Tiger."

North America; however, Mississippi is within the traditional range of the Florida panther. Within the last two years a deer feeder's game camera recorded a night photo of a panther in central Louisiana.

I have been asked several times if there is any historical record of the wildlife encountered by the first settlers of this area. There actually are old accounts—and they hold some surprises.

Wolf Road (now sometimes called Wolfe Road) in northeast Lowndes County received its name because of the large number of wolves in the area when it was settled during the early 1820s. White Slough, on the island by the Columbus-Lowndes Port, was a favorite hunting ground for both the Choctaws and the first Euro-American settlers in Columbus. In an 1870 interview, Peter Pitchlynn recalled bear hunting when he resided on Redbud Creek (southwest of Artesia and southeast of Starkville) during the 1820s. Today there are believed to be just over one hundred bears in Mississippi.

One of the most interesting accounts is described in the notebook of George Rapalji, which can be found at the Mississippi Department of Archives and History. Rapalji was a trapper and fur trader along the Big Black River (which flows from Webster County to the Mississippi River south of Vicksburg) between 1786 and 1797. He recorded the following skins being traded: deer, otter, bear, raccoon, fox, beaver, cat, wildcat and "tyger." Over the course of his nine years of trapping and trading on the Big Black, Rapalji only reported one tyger skin as having been taken. That skin was taken in 1794 and was possibly a jaguar.

Until the late 1700s, the range of the jaguar (which was then known as the *tyger*, *el tigre* or *American tiger*) extended to the Red River in eastern Texas and Louisiana. There are also several accounts of it being seen east of the Mississippi River. In *Wildlife in America*, Peter Matthiessen quotes a 1711 account from coastal Carolina as saying, "Tygers are more to the westward." Additionally, he refers to a 1737 sighting of a tyger in Carolina. The three different types of cat skins taken in Mississippi during the 1790s by Rapalji may well represent bobcats, Florida panthers and jaguars.

As to the black panther, I have my own idea. While deer hunting near Artesia around 1980, I watched as a pair of panthers crossed the edge of a field late one afternoon. One was tawny-colored and the other was brownish. I watched them for about five minutes, and as the light faded the brown one began to appear to be black.

HUNTING'S ROOTS RUN DEEP

I have several friends who believe that there are three important holidays each year: Christmas, opening day of deer season and opening day of turkey season. The roots of hunting run deep in the South. References to hunting are included in the earliest accounts of the settlement of the Columbus area.

The fur trade records of George Rapalji, who operated along the Big Black River during the 1790s, show the abundance of wildlife in what is now Mississippi. Choctaw Indian trade records from along the Tombigbee in 1807 reflect the animal furs they were trading and included deer, beaver, otter, fox, raccoon, cat and bear.

Two early residents who told of their hunting exploits were Peter Pitchlynn, who was born on the banks of the Noxubee River in 1806, and Gideon Lincecum, who moved from Tuscaloosa to the Columbus area in 1818.

During the 1820s, Pitchlynn lived in a log house on the south end of a prairie that ran from west of the present-day Golden Triangle Airport to a few miles south of Artesia. By the early 1830s that prairie was known as Peter Pitchlynn's Prairie. In an 1870 interview in the *Atlantic Monthly*, Pitchlynn

A circa 1890s photograph of a hunting camp near Columbus.

recounted how he enjoyed bear hunting. That would have been in Catalpa Creek, which bordered the prairie on the west. Gideon Lincecum also told of bear hunting and wrote a number of descriptions of hunts.

Lincecum related how many people would hunt bears armed only with knives. In the early 1800s the forests around Columbus were home to many wolves, natural enemies of the bear. Hunters led by a pack of dogs would pursue bears. The bear would ignore the human hunters to attack the dogs, associating them with wolves. That enabled the hunters to jump on the bear and kill it with a knife while it was preoccupied with the dogs. Lincecum told how the most dangerous aspect of the hunt was not the bear, but a hunter armed with a gun who might accidentally shoot another hunter.

Lincecum especially enjoyed deer hunting. The first deer he recalled shooting around Columbus was a big buck he shot in 1818 near what is now the intersection of Main and Market Streets in downtown Columbus.

White Slough (on the island north of the Columbus-Lowndes Port) was Lincecum's favorite hunting grounds. He said that the Choctaws called it *Shonk Colocherocoby* or "Crooked Cypress." Lincecum wrote, "In the canebrake and all around the cypress swamp could be found more turkeys and deer, and some bear, coons, foxes, panthers and catamounts than at any place I ever lived." He also found that during the winter the slough filled up with ducks and geese. Lincecum hunted both to provide food for his family and to obtain venison to smoke for shipment to markets in Mobile.

The White Slough area had long been a hunting ground. An interesting artifact was found when the new river channel was being cut through the west end of White Slough for the Tenn-Tom Waterway. It was a two-thousand-year-old cypress knee with an Indian spear point embedded in it.

For those who wish to read Lincecum's actual accounts, they are found in Jerry Bryan Lincecum's and Edward Hake Phillips's *Adventures of a Frontier Naturalist: The Life and Times of Dr. Gideon Lincecum.*

A PASSING DISTANT THUNDER

On the Natchez Trace, not far below Mathiston, one passes a historic marker for Pigeon Roost and Pigeon Roost Creek. It was the home of the Folsoms, a prominent Choctaw family in the late 1700s and early 1800s. Those who stop to read the marker also learn a bit of all-but-forgotten natural history. The marker tells how Pigeon Roost Creek is "a reminder of the millions of migrating passenger pigeons that once roosted in trees in this area."

The passenger pigeon was an American bird once so numerous that the passing overhead of a flock was said to blacken the sky for hours or, even by a few accounts, days. John Audubon described the sound of an approaching flock of pigeons as "the sound of distant thunder." In the 1820s their numbers were estimated at between three and five billion, but they could not withstand senseless slaughter, habitat destruction and a disruption of their roosting. In the 1850s people were still in awe of their sheer numbers as the birds migrated. That was not to last, though, as by the 1870s articles began appearing about the quickly diminishing size of the passing flocks.

The last confirmed wild passenger pigeon was shot and killed on March 24, 1900, and the last known living one died at the Cincinnati Zoo in 1914. The rapid passing of the birds is one of the more disturbing stories of American natural history. It is a story that, as evidenced by Pigeon Roost near Mathiston, is as much local as it is national.

A passenger pigeon drawn by Alexander Wilson, engraved by W.H. Lizars and published in 1832. Lizars is noted as the engraver of some of Audubon's most famous elephant folio birds.

The passenger pigeon had long been in our area. Among the Choctaw and Chickasaw Indians of Mississippi it was exceeded in importance only by the turkey. The wild pigeon roosts were gathering places for Native American hunters during the roosting season when the huge flocks were present. The Indians mentioned the bird eggs as an especially popular food.

In the late 1700s and very early 1800s there was not the heavy pressure of over hunting or habitat loss to threaten the wild pigeon population. While traveling through Alabama in 1818, Gideon Lincecum wrote, "The entire forest was alive with wild pigeons but nobody troubled them." To the Indians and early settlers, passenger pigeons were a source of food, not the subject of senseless slaughter.

The migrations of the pigeons must have been a sight to behold. An 1821 report described flocks of pigeons as being tens of miles long. A later description told of the birds flying for long periods "at the rate of a mile in a minute." Because millions of birds would roost in a single location, surrounding crops and forest were decimated. The 1890 edition of *The Encyclopedia Britannica* recorded that, at one time, "Passenger-Pigeons so swarmed and ravaged the colonists' crops near Montreal that a bishop of his own church was constrained to exorcise them with holy water, as if they had been demons."

Audubon observed the damage done to a forest that had served as a roost: "Many trees...were broken off at no great distance from the ground, and the branches of many of the largest and tallest had given way, as if the forest had been swept by a tornado."

Perhaps Audubon's most telling description was of the slaughter of the birds at a roost on the Green River in Kentucky: "A great number of persons with horses, and wagons, guns and ammunition" had arrived from as far away as one hundred miles. Two farmers even brought three hundred hogs to feed on the birds. The armed rabble shot birds and struck at birds with poles and continued their assault on the roost through the night, with the forest lit by huge bonfires. Audubon also recalled a hunt in Pennsylvania where a single man with a net caught and killed over five hundred dozen birds in one day.

Such slaughter and the cutting of the great forest had their effect. Flocks of millions of pigeons were still reported in the 1850s, but an account written twenty-five years later reported that "possibly the number of wild pigeons is decreasing." By the 1880s they were uncommon and by the 1890s they were rare, but by 1900, wild passenger pigeons were no more. Passenger pigeons had gone from a population of billions to extinction in a period of less than seventy-five years.

In 1854, when there were still huge populations of wild pigeons, an article in *Arthur's Illustrated Home Magazine* stated, "The Americans may be truly called the passenger pigeons of a new civilization."

Now that is a frightening comparison.

Turkey Hunting and the Settlement of Columbus

Turkey season will soon open, and hunters wearing the latest camo and carrying their favorite turkey calls will venture into the woods. The tradition of turkey hunting in the Tombigbee Valley goes back to the early Native

An engraving of turkey hunting from the November 11, 1854 issue of *Gleason's Pictorial.*

Americans who were here even before the historic period. Artifacts found at prehistoric Indian campsites often include turkey bones.

For southeastern Indians, turkeys were more than just a food and feather source. The turkey was often associated with warriors and warfare. Gobbler spurs were used as arrow points, and an imitation of a turkey gobble was even used as a war cry.

Gideon Lincecum moved from Georgia to Tuscaloosa in 1816 and then to what became Columbus in 1818. He moved to Texas during the 1840s. He enjoyed turkey hunting and often wrote about his hunts in Alabama, Mississippi and Texas.

Lincecum often used the leaf of a wild peach for a turkey call. In describing one hunt he wrote, "I had the leaf of a wild peach, a most excellent leaf to yelp with, and I had been admiring how well I had been speaking Turkey with it." He also found that the leaf of the elder was good for making a soft yelp.

Lincecum's favorite hunting ground was "White Slue," which is now the south part of the island across from Columbus. He described how in the slough's canebrakes and cypress swamps could be found more game (including turkeys) "than at any place I ever lived."

It was in 1818 that Lincecum made a camp on the banks of the Tombigbee River near the present site of the Columbus Marina. At sunset on his first night on the Tombigbee, he heard "heavy turkeys flying up to roost a little distance out." There appeared to be at least forty turkeys alighting in the trees, so Lincecum was out at daybreak hunting them.

At first light, he saw a huge turkey "on a low limb, not more than thirty feet from the ground." Lincecum shot the large turkey and carried it back to his camp. He noted that the turkey's "weight when dressed was twenty-nine and a half pounds." Before the year was gone he observed many other turkeys just as large.

The next day, Lincecum's wife said to him, "You have found the right place for us to stop at...who could look at this fat game, so easily obtained, this beautiful river with its handsome dry bluff and gushing spring water and think otherwise." Thus is the relationship between turkey hunting and the settlement of Columbus.

Lincecum's hunting accounts can be found in *Adventures of a Frontier Naturalist*.

Chapter 3

THE PEOPLE

WHERE WAS DAVY CROCKETT?

I grew up watching Walt Disney presenting Davy Crockett as bigger than life. Little did I realize then that one of his exploits took place around Tuscaloosa or that he traveled to Fort Smith at John Pitchlynn's Plymouth Bluff residence for supplies.

In the summer of 1813 violence broke out across the Mississippi Territory, which included present-day Alabama. A civil war erupted in the Creek Indian Nation, and the British, as part of the War of 1812, encouraged the Creek Red Stick faction to attack settlers.

On July 27 at Burnt Corn Creek, territorial militia attacked Creek Indians as they returned from British-occupied Spanish Pensacola with munitions and supplies. Then, on August 30, 1813, Red Stick Creeks attacked Fort Mims (above Mobile), burning the fort and killing over 250 settlers and their Creek Indian allies. In late 1813, Tennessee Militia, including David Crockett, marched on the Creek village at the falls of the Warrior River (Tuscaloosa) but found it deserted. Crockett fought in several actions against the Creek in early 1814 but returned home to south Tennessee when his enlistment was up.

October 1814 found General Andrew Jackson in Mobile, where he was expecting the British to attack. (In January 1815 the British did attack, but the main fighting took place at New Orleans.) Jackson was also concerned that

An engraving of David Crockett during the Creek Indian War phase of the War of 1812. This is an illustration from an 1860 copy of Crockett's autobiography, *Life of Col David Crockett by Himself.*

the British had occupied Spanish Pensacola and were using it as a base. In need of reinforcements, Jackson ordered the five-thousand-man Tennessee Militia to come south and join him.

General John Coffee led Tennessee's Second Brigade of three thousand men down the Natchez Trace to the Chickasaw villages (Tupelo). From there they traveled south down Gaines Old Trace to John Pitchlynn's (Plymouth Bluff at the west bank of the Columbus Lock and Dam) where the troops were provided with corn. At Pitchlynn's was a fortified blockhouse called Fort Smith. Beef was to be obtained at Middleton Mackey's residence thirty miles south on the Noxubee River (Macon). It was probably General Coffee's trek through the area that led to the myth of Andrew Jackson marching through Columbus on his way to the Battle of New Orleans.

On October 14, 1814, General Coffee wrote Andrew Jackson from "Peachland's" (as he called Pitchlynn's) that Russell's company was about a week behind the army and that St. Stephens Trace, which ran south from Pitchlynn's toward Mobile, was expected to be a better road than the one on which they had traveled. Before Russell's company arrived, Coffee had already headed south to join with Jackson near Mobile.

One of Russell's scouts, who also would have stopped and received supplies at Pitchlynn's, was one David Crockett. In his autobiography Crockett wrote, "An army was to be raised to go to Pensacola, and I determined to go with them, for I wanted a small taste of British fighting." Crockett continued, noting that he joined with Major Russell's company but "couldn't start with the main army but followed on a little time after them." Crockett left out the fact that they had been serving as General Coffee's scouts and were traveling a week behind the army. On November 7, 1814, Jackson, whose troops included John Pitchlynn and Choctaw warriors, stormed and captured Pensacola. Major Russell's company did not arrive on the scene until, as Crockett put it, "a little after the feast."

After the capture of Pensacola, General Coffee and most of the army headed to New Orleans to meet the British. A smaller force, including Russell's company, remained in the Pensacola-Mobile area to mop up the remaining Creek resistance.

Somehow I just don't recall the part in the Disney movie *King of the Wild Frontier* where Crockett, though a scout, gets left behind by the army and misses the battle.

A Long Dangerous Ride

We are all familiar with Paul Revere's famous ride and Longfellow's poem describing how Revere was "ready to ride."

Ready to ride and spread the alarm
Through every Middlesex village and farm,
For the country folk to be up and to arm.

However, few people are aware of the ride of Samuel Edmondson in September 1813. All he did was ride 450 miles through Indian territory to spread the alarm that the Creek Indians had massacred the settlement at Fort Mims and were attacking other settlements along the Tombigbee and Alabama Rivers.

In 1811, the famed Shawnee leader Tecumseh visited the southeastern Indian nations to try to form an Indian alliance. Though rejected by the Chickasaws and Choctaws, his ideas found favor among the Creek Indians

An 1858 engraving of the Fort Mims massacre that occurred in 1813.

of central Alabama. Then, 1812 saw war break out between the United States and Great Britain. The British attempted to incite Native Americans to attack the United States' settlements in the West.

Violence began to erupt. On July 27, 1813, Mississippi territorial militia attacked a party of Creek Indians returning from Pensacola with munitions supplied by the British. Then, on August 30, the Creek Indians attacked the American settlement at Fort Mims. They killed over 250 men, women and children and burned the fort.

The next day, U.S. Choctaw Factor George Gaines realized the settlement's grave danger. He asked Samuel Edmondson to carry letters to Nashville requesting help from Andrew Jackson and Tennessee Governor Blunt. Edmondson agreed and was given letters that appealed to General Jackson "to march down with his brigade of mounted men and save the Tombigbee settlements."

Gaines provided Edmondson with a fast horse and told him to ride day and night. Gaines also provided him with letters of warning addressed to influential people who lived along Edmondson's route. The letters also asked that each person furnish Edmondson with provisions and their best horse.

Those providing assistance included Charles Juzan (present-day Lauderdale Springs), William Starnes (Macon), John Pitchlynn (Plymouth Bluff) and George James (Egypt). The route taken was St. Sephens Trace, which connected St. Stephens with John Pitchlynn's residence and roughly followed what is now Highway 45. From Pitchlynn's, the route continued north to the Chickasaw villages (now Tupelo) and then up the Natchez Trace to Nashville.

Edmondson met with Governor Blunt and Andrew Jackson immediately after he arrived in Nashville. When Jackson read Gaines's letter, he began pacing the floor and replied, "By the eternal these people must be saved." In fact, Jackson was soon riding (in a buggy due a dueling wound) south at the head of the Tennessee Militia to defend the Tombigbee settlements.

Edmondson eventually settled in Lowndes County, southeast of Columbus. He died in 1869 and is buried in an old church cemetery off of Highway 69 South.

Colonel Wilfred Beaver: "A Patrol Leader of Great Dash"

Growing up in Columbus, I knew Colonel Beaver simply as a family friend and former World War I pilot. Little did I realize that he was another of those Columbus residents who, though not well known locally, left a huge footprint on the world.

Wilfred Beaver was born in England in 1897 and, after graduating from high school, went to Canada to study dentistry in 1914. World War I erupted before he could begin his studies, so he joined the Canadian army and soon wound up in a field artillery battery. After two years on the Western Front, he was allowed to join the British Royal Flying Corps. It was there that he first left his mark.

After completing flight training he was assigned to the famous No. 20 Squadron of the Royal Flying Corps. Second Lieutenant Beaver joined the squadron on October 22, 1917, in St. Marie Chappelle, France. He made five practice flights and on October 27 flew his first combat mission. On November 13, he shot down his first German plane.

Beaver saw extensive action, flying as many as three combat patrols in a day. Between October 27, 1917, and June 12, 1918, he was credited with nineteen victories over German aircraft.

Captain Wilfred Beaver of the famous No. 20 Squadron of the Royal Flying Corps was awarded the British Military Cross at Buckingham Palace by King George V in 1918. *Courtesy of Mickey Brislin.*

Beaver's grandson, Mickey Brislin, recalls the story of when his grandfather's plane was shot up by Freiherr von Richthofen, the "Red Baron." Beaver's plane had been badly damaged, and Richthofen signaled him to fly toward his home base. When Beaver arrived back over his base Richthofen circled behind him and opened fire again, forcing Beaver to crash-land.

That may have happened on March 25, 1918, as Beaver crashed that day and his squadron had been in combat against Richthofen around that time. On the twenty-seventh, Captains Kirkman and Hedley of Beaver's squadron were shot down by Richthofen. Richthofen was shot down and killed three weeks later, and Beaver told of attending his funeral.

Beaver's last patrol was on June 12, at which time he was a captain and flight leader. That day he led twelve British Bristol aircraft on a bombing mission when they were jumped by German fighters. Beaver was wounded and his observer was killed. In spite of his wounds and the damage to his plane, Beaver managed to make it back to his home base. However, he was hospitalized because of his wounds and did not return to combat.

On June 22, 1918, the *London Gazette* reported that Captain Wilfred Beaver had been awarded the British Military Cross. Beaver had received a telegram that read: "Your attendance is required at Oxford Buckingham Palace on Saturday next the nineteenth instant at ten o'clock am. Service dress please." It was signed Lord Chamberlain. King George V presented Beaver with the Military Cross at Buckingham Palace.

The citation recognized his aerial victories and accomplishments and stated, "He has displayed marked gallantry and resource and has proved himself a patrol leader of great dash and ability."

In 1919, he immigrated to the United States. He became a naturalized citizen on September 26, 1926. In June 1942 he enlisted in the U.S. Army Air Corps as a captain. In 1943 he was a major and executive officer of the 447 Bomb Group of the Eighth Air Force in England. There he developed what would be a lifelong friendship with Air Force general Curtis LeMay. By the end of World War II he was a lieutenant colonel commanding the 447 Bomb group. He left active duty in January 1946 with the rank of colonel.

While Beaver was with the 447, his daughter Pat met and married Mickey Brislin Sr., who was serving with the Bomb Group. Beaver and Brislin were working with Bruce Lumber Company and came to Columbus with the large Bruce operation that was once here. Brislin later entered the air conditioning business, and the family merged into the life of Columbus with most townspeople not knowing the legendary story of Colonel Beaver. He died in 1986 and is buried in Memorial Gardens in Columbus.

RUBE BURROWS: THE MOST FEARED TRAIN ROBBER

Rube Burrows was called "The King of the Outlaws" by some publications. Though his exploits were limited to Alabama, Mississippi, Arkansas and Texas, his fame and notoriety were nationwide. He became the most feared train robber of the late 1880s.

Burrows was born in 1855, near the small Lamar County, Alabama community of Jewel. There his father was a farmer and, on occasion, a

A gunfight between Rube Burrows and a sheriff's posse in Blount County, Alabama, as pictured on the cover of the November 16, 1889 issue of *Frank Leslie's Illustrated Newspaper*.

schoolteacher. Burrows lived there until the mid-1870s, when he moved to Texas. In later years, when hotly pursued by law enforcement or railroad detectives, he would return to Lamar County to hide out.

In Texas, he worked on his uncle's ranch and got married. Burrows seemed to change when his wife died in 1880. He sent his children back to Alabama with his brother while he remained in Texas. Burrows became a successful cattleman, though he seemed to acquire many head of cattle under suspicious circumstance. He even remarried, but the relationship did not last.

Restless and inspired by stories of Jesse James and Sam Bass, Burrows robbed his first train in Texas in 1886. There followed at least eight other train robberies in Texas, Arkansas, Alabama and Mississippi—and the murder of the postmaster in Jewel, Alabama. In Mississippi, trains were robbed at Duck Hill in Montgomery County and Buckatunna in Jones County.

Accounts of Burrows's robberies spread nationwide. The New York *Country Gentleman* reported in 1889 that "Rube Burrows, a desperate outlaw, is terrorizing Blount County, Ala. Houses are locked and guarded, children kept at home, and even churches are closed." The *New York Times* reported that after Burrows's Buckatunna robbery, "a reward of $7,500 was then offered for his capture dead or alive."

Burrows kept his gang small, and the robberies were committed by only Burrows and one or two accomplices. By 1890 his small gang was beginning to break up. Joe Jackson, who had ridden with Burrows from the beginning, was captured by railroad detectives and Columbus, Mississippi police at the Southern Railway (C&G) passenger depot on Main Street in Columbus. Another gang member, Rube Smith, was captured at the Frisco depot in Amory.

In October 1890, members of a posse that had been chasing Burrows were told of his location, and he was captured near Linden, Alabama. He was carried to Linden but managed to escape. He was then shot and killed by J.D. Carter, a member of the posse, during a gunfight in the street beside the courthouse in Linden.

Although little known now, Burrows's exploits were legendary around the turn of the century. Several books about his life appeared, and among those interested in the history of western outlaws, his story continued to be told. An Emmy-winning television series by Republic Pictures in 1954–55 featured accounts of Jesse James, Billy the Kid, Black Bart, Doc Holliday and Rube Burrows. In 1966, Leaf issued bubble gum cards of the most famous "Bad Guys." Rube Burrows was included.

Rube Burrows, "King of the Outlaws," once walked the streets of Vernon, Sulligent, Columbus, Carrollton and other area towns. One of his hideouts was even said to have been the Dismals, which is now a popular nature area in northwest Alabama.

VISIONS OF FORT APACHE AND TENNESSEE WILLIAMS

I was recently asked if I knew the name of the doctor who delivered Tennessee Williams when he was born in Columbus in 1911. There is no birth certificate of Williams to provide the doctor's name. That question, however, brings to mind visions of Fort Apache, the Spanish-American War, the Panama Canal and Dr. Walter Reed. They all share a common thread with the birth of Tennessee Williams.

William Richards was born in Columbus, Mississippi, in 1871. He was a descendant of a prominent early Columbus family. He attended medical school and, after graduation, enlisted in the cavalry, where he served as a surgeon at Fort Apache at the close of the Indian War. He then served during the Spanish-American War. He was an assistant surgeon under Dr. Walter Reed and worked on yellow fever patients in Panama at the start of the canal construction. After leaving the military, he returned to Columbus, where he opened a medical practice and attended St. Paul's Episcopal Church. The Richards family was friends with Reverend Walter Dakin (grandfather of Tennessee) and his family. Although his specialty was ear, nose, and throat, Dr. Richards had a general practice background and found that his friends called on him for all of their family medical needs.

The Columbus City Directory of 1912 gives 618 Main Street as the address of Dr. Richards's office. That was the location of the McKinley Sanitarium and later the Doster Hospital. Dr. Richards retired around 1925 and moved with his family to Ocean Springs. During the early 1950s he returned to the Columbus area, moving to a family farm near Artesia.

In *Tom: The Unknown Tennessee Williams*, author Lyle Leverich relates that, in 1941, Tennessee wrote in his journal that he had taken a "bike trip" from New Orleans to the Mississippi coast to "join Bill Richards and his family." Tennessee described Bill Richards as "Bill who is the son of the Doctor who brought me into this world." Dr. Richards's son, William, was

A circa 1910 postcard of the McKinley Sanitarium. Its former site is now home to the Trustmark Bank on Main Street in Columbus.

an early friend and longtime acquaintance of Tennessee, who called him Bill. A member of the Richards family recalls an occasion prior to World War II when Tennessee Williams rode his bicycle from New Orleans to their house in Ocean Springs for a visit. Another family member recalls going to a restaurant (Begge's) in New York with William Richards around 1963. Tennessee was there and, upon seeing them enter the restaurant, called them to his table. The restaurant appeared to be a gathering place for Tennessee and his friends.

The historical record shows Dr. William Richards to be the doctor who delivered Tennessee Williams in Columbus at the McKinley Sanitarium in 1911.

I remember Dr. Richards as a most gracious gentleman who continued to hunt and fish into his nineties. He had great respect for Native Americans and objected to the way in which they were portrayed in the movies of the 1950s. He would often conclude an especially good meal by saying that he had had "an elegant sufficiency." Dr. William Richards died in 1967, leaving a rich legacy of accomplishments and experiences that most people can only dream of. Oh, and Tennessee Williams was not the most interesting person Dr. Richards knew, for when serving in the cavalry, he met Geronimo.

ABERDEEN'S REVEREND INGRAHAM AND CECIL B. DEMILLE'S *THE TEN COMMANDMENTS*

Recently, Aberdeen attorney T.W. Pace sent me a copy of Reverend J. Lundy Sykes's history of St. John's Episcopal Church in Aberdeen. I found this interesting because Reverend Sykes had married my parents and because the history contained much information on Reverend Joseph Holt Ingraham, who had been rector of St. John's Church during the early 1850s. What was not in the history was the role Reverend Ingraham played in Cecil B. DeMille's classic movie *The Ten Commandments*.

Ingraham experienced life as few others have. He was born into a shipbuilding family in Portland, Maine, in 1809. As a teenager, he sailed to South America on one of his grandfather's ships. There he became involved in a revolution.

He returned to New England and entered Yale College, although he did not graduate. In 1830 he ventured to New Orleans, where he studied law. There he showed little interest in the legal profession and again moved. Ingraham began teaching at Jefferson College in Washington, Mississippi, just outside Natchez. Though he had never graduated from Yale, he was still given the title of "Professor."

He began writing novels while teaching at Jefferson College. In an 1836 review, Edgar Allan Poe called Ingraham's work overly descriptive with unnecessary detail. Ingraham soon became a prolific writer. An 1846 letter to Henry Wadsworth Longfellow mentions that he has written eighty books. Again, though, Ingraham became restless.

He decided to study for the ministry and moved to Nashville in 1849. There he founded a school for young girls and studied theology under his brother, the rector of Christ Episcopal Church. He returned to Natchez in 1851 and was ordained a deacon by Episcopal Bishop W.M. Green. The following year he became a priest.

In 1851 he was sent to the struggling Episcopal congregation at Aberdeen, where efforts to build a church had raised only $1,250. Ingraham responded by becoming architect, contractor and laborer. He completed the building in 1853 with the assistance of two young men and nine slaves. It is still in use today as St. John's Church.

Ingraham resigned from his position in 1853 and devoted more time to writing. He also helped with church services in Mobile and at St. Paul's in Columbus. In 1859, he wrote *The Pillar of Fire or Israel in Bondage*, which

THE

PILLAR OF FIRE;

OR,

Israel in Bondage.

BY REV. J. H. INGRAHAM, .
Rector of Christ Church, and of St. Thomas' Hall, Holly Springs, Miss.

AUTHOR OF
"THE PRINCE OF THE HOUSE OF DAVID."

NEW-YORK:
PUDNEY & RUSSELL, PUBLISHERS,
79 JOHN-STREET.
BLAKEMAN & MASON,
310 BROADWAY.

1859.

Title page to Reverend J.H. Ingraham's 1859 book, *The Pillar of Fire.*

was widely read and remained popular into the twentieth century. In 1858, Ingraham accepted the position as rector of Christ Church in Holly Springs. He died there as the result of a shooting accident in 1860.

All of this begs the question, "What did Ingraham have to do with a classic Hollywood movie filmed ninety-six years after he died?" In the movie's credits, the third name shown (behind only Cecil B. DeMille and assistant director Henry Wilcoxon) was a writing credit to J.H. Ingraham. Apparently, much of the screenplay was taken from *Pillar of Fire*. It may well be that the over descriptiveness and detail that Edgar Allan Poe did not care for in Ingraham's work made it attractive years later as a screenplay. So, ninety-six years after he died, Joseph Holt Ingraham, former rector of St. John's Episcopal Church in Aberdeen, received a top billing for the classic movie *The Ten Commandments*.

A *TITANIC* COLUMBUS LINK

Many know that this year marked the 100th anniversary of the sinking of the *Titanic*, but few know of Columbus's link to this incident. Dr. John D. Richards grew up in Columbus, went to medical school and then moved to New York City around the turn of the century. While in New York he became prominent as a physician, polo player and trainer of polo ponies. In a 1910 article, the *New York Times* referred to him as a surgeon at St. Mark's Hospital. His patients included members of the Rockefeller, Straus, Colt and Barrymore families. After he retired from practice, he and his wife, Marcella Billups Richards, returned to Columbus to reside in her family home at 905 Main Street.

The *Titanic* struck an iceberg on April 14, 1912, and sank around 2:30 a.m. on April 15. The ship was carrying with it some 1,517 souls. Among the lost were Mr. and Mrs. Isidor Straus, who Dr. Richards said were his "good friends." When the ship was sinking, Mr. Straus had refused to enter a lifeboat before any other man, and Mrs. Straus refused to leave his side. They were both lost, but their story of love and loyalty has lived on in every movie made about the *Titanic*.

The *Carpathia* rescued some 705 survivors and carried them to New York. Dr. Richards was one of the physicians called to meet the ship at the dock to tend to those who had survived. One hundred years ago, on April 18, 1912, the *Carpathia* arrived in the New York Harbor with those who had survived.

Dr. Richards described the scene as "surreal." Thousands of people gathered at the pier where the *Carpathia* was expected to dock. Many were trying to get information on family and friends. Others just came to gawk at the spectacle. The rescue ship arrived in the harbor at about 7:00 p.m. Before docking, the ship unloaded the *Titanic*'s lifeboats. Dr. Richards recalled that his most vivid impression was that of the workers trying to sand the name *Titanic* off of the lifeboats. After the *Carpathia* docked, he was able to pass through the crowd. He was one of the first to board the *Carpathia* to tend to those in need.

I can remember Dr. Richards showing me his copy of Walter Lord's book on the *Titanic*, *A Night to Remember*, and saying that it was an accurate account of what happened as experienced by the survivors.

Folder found in Mrs. John D. Richards's scrapbook containing the deck plan of the *Carpathia.*

CLYDE KILBY AND HIS COLUMBUS "HOBBIT HOLE"

Clyde Kilby's book, *Tolkien & the Silmarillion*, begins, "I first met J.R.R. Tolkien late on the afternoon of September 1, 1964." As chairman of the English department of Wheaton College, Kilby was a leading scholar and author on Tolkien, with whom he spent a summer working, and C.S. Lewis, with whom he corresponded for many years.

Clyde Kilby was born in Johnson City, Tennessee, in 1902. In 1930 he married Martha Harris of Columbus at her family's North Side home. When he retired in 1981, he and Martha moved back to the home in Columbus, where he lived until his death in 1986. Few people in Columbus were aware, then or now, of his close ties to two of the twentieth century's greatest writers.

In Columbus, the Kilbys were described as "delightful, wonderful people." Clyde even hosted a Columbus study group on C.S. Lewis. When inviting

A drawing of the Columbus home where Clyde and Martha Kilby were married and later lived. The drawing was done by Oscar-winning Disney animator Josh Meador. *Drawing courtesy of Billups-Garth Archives, Columbus-Lowndes Public Library. Gift of Phil Meador.*

people into his Columbus home, Kilby often referred to it as his "hobbit hole."

Kilby became interested in the work of C.S. Lewis in 1943. He met Lewis in 1953 and continued to correspond with him until his death. Included in the *Letters of C.S. Lewis* (edited by Lewis's brother, W.H. Lewis) are several letters from Lewis to Kilby. Kilby is considered one of the foremost biographers of Lewis. Books he authored or coauthored on Lewis include *Christian World of C.S. Lewis, A Mind Awake: An Anthology of C.S. Lewis, Images of Salvation in the Fiction of C.S. Lewis* and *C.S. Lewis: Images of His World.*

It was with J.R.R. Tolkien, though, that Kilby worked most closely. He first met Tolkien in 1964 and spent the summer of 1966 working with Tolkien at his home. Kilby spent that summer reading and critically discussing with Tolkien his Silmarillion manuscript.

Kilby became a leading scholar and lecturer on the Inklings, an informal literary group that met at the Eagle and Child Pub in Oxford, England, during the 1930s and '40s. The group included Tolkien, Lewis, G.K. Chesterton, Charles Williams and several others. The award for Inkling studies has been named the Clyde S. Kilby Award in his honor.

In 1966, Kilby was instrumental in the establishment of the Marion E. Wade Center at Wheaton College in Illinois. The center contains a major collection of works and materials associated with Lewis, Tolkien and other British authors, including several Inklings. The collection includes Tolkien's desk and Lewis's old family wardrobe.

WILLIAM COCKE LIVED THE FOUNDING OF AMERICA

One of the most interesting figures in Columbus history was William Cocke. He was born in Virginia in 1747 and died in Columbus in 1828. Cocke actually lived the founding and settlement of the United States. He then became one of the founders of Columbus.

Few experienced the beginnings of this country in the way that Cocke did. He studied and then practiced law, but he left his mark in many different fields. He participated in the tarring and feathering of an English recruiting officer in 1774 and, in 1776, led four companies of Virginia militia into Tennessee to fight against "hostile Indians."

Cocke then had the unusual distinction in 1778 and 1779 of representing Washington County in the Virginia Assembly and the North Carolina House of Burgesses at the same time. He knew Daniel Boone and was associated with him in the settlement of Boonesboro.

During the American Revolution, Cocke served as a captain and one of the "Overmountain Men" under Colonel John Sevier in the 1780 American victory over British Colonel Ferguson at the Battle of King's Mountain. He also saw action at the Battles of Long Island Flats and Fort Thicketty. Another of Columbus's founders, Silas McBee, was also present at the Battle of King's Mountain.

Cocke continued his association with John Sevier after the Revolution and was one of the foremost proponents of the state of Franklin, which later evolved into the state of Tennessee. Upon Tennessee's statehood, he became one of the new state's first two U.S. senators.

In November 1792, Cocke wrote a very long letter to the Nashville newspaper that was uncomplimentary of the Cherokee Indians. In response, Cherokee Chief Hanging Maw wrote a very short letter to the newspaper. That letter mentioned Cocke's "long letter" and, in effect, said, "he who must talk long must not be talking the truth."

Cocke's first wife, Mary Maclin, died in 1795. A year later he married Kissiah Sims. Cocke became friends with Andrew Jackson in Tennessee. He became judge of the First Circuit in 1809. Political disagreements almost led to Cocke and Jackson fighting a duel. Mutual friends intervened to prevent the possibly deadly confrontation.

The Creek Indian War, which was a combination of a Creek civil war and the southern phase of the War of 1812, erupted in the summer of 1813. Fear struck the state of Tennessee and the Mississippi Territory when, on August 30, 1813, Creek Indians attacked and overran Fort Mims on the Alabama River. Over 250 American settlers and friendly Indians were killed in the massacre. Andrew Jackson responded by leading "his brigade of mounted men" south to "save the Tombigbee settlements" in what is now south Alabama.

Although sixty-five, Cocke volunteered and enlisted as a private to serve under Jackson. In his January 29, 1814 report of actions against the Creeks, Jackson favorably mentioned Cocke. The two men later reconciled. Later, in 1814, Cocke was appointed U.S. agent to the Chickasaw Nation. He served in that role until late 1817. By 1819 he was living in the new town of Columbus. His wife, Kissiah, died in 1820 and was buried in the "Tombigbee Graveyard," which was the river bluff just north of where "Riverview" is located.

Columbus was chartered as a town by the state of Mississippi on February 10, 1821. Commissioners were appointed to lay out the town of Columbus and to effectively serve as the town's first governing body. At their June 4, 1821 meeting, William Cocke was elected president. He also served in the Mississippi legislature, giving him the rare distinction of having served in the legislative bodies of four different states.

Cocke's home in Columbus was a two-story, cross-hall dogtrot that stood where the Tennessee Williams Welcome Center now is. The first license to operate an inn or tavern in Columbus was granted to Cocke. It was to operate in his house.

One of Cocke's children, stepson Barlett Sims, was sheriff of Marion County, Alabama, in 1819 (when Columbus was believed to be in Alabama) and then Monroe County, Mississippi, in 1821. In Columbus, his son Stephen was clerk of the county court, while his stepson Matthew Sims served as the deputy clerk.

From Daniel Boone to Andrew Jackson to the founding of Columbus, William Cocke lived American history. He died in Columbus in 1828. His grave can be found in Friendship Cemetery.

CAPTAIN SAM KAYE'S "ACROBATIC EASTER EGG"

On June 15, 1919, the *Columbus Dispatch* reported that Captain Sam Kaye had arrived home from France. The article described Kaye as returning home "decorated with the Distinguished Service Cross, bestowed on him by his own government for bravery in action, and with the Croix de Guerre, bestowed by the French government for exceptional prowess in the air."

Samuel Kaye, a Columbus native, enlisted in the U.S. Army Air Service at the start of World War I. He was sent to the Aviation Field School at Austin, Texas, and then to flight training at Chanute Field in Illinois. He was ordered to Europe and arrived in England in November 1917.

Kaye's first assignment was as a ferry pilot flying between Paris and London. Then, on July 9, 1918, he was assigned to the Ninety-fourth Aero Squadron, First Pursuit Group, at Saints, France. The Ninety-fourth was known as the "Hat in the Ring" Squadron and was under the command of Captain Eddie Rickenbacker, America's top ace of World War I.

Captain Sam Kaye of the "Hat in the Ring" Squadron and his Spad airplane, which he called his "Acrobatic Easter Egg." *Courtesy of Pat Kaye.*

Rickenbacker and Kaye became lifelong friends. After the war, Rickenbacker, who founded Eastern Airlines, would come to Columbus to visit Kaye.

Kaye was awarded his first Distinguished Service Cross for action over the region of Epinonville, France, on September 29, 1918. Lieutenants Kaye and Reed Chambers attacked a formation of six German planes, shooting down one and forcing the others to retire back to German lines.

The citation for Kaye's second Distinguished Service Cross reads:

> *The President of the United States of America, authorized by Act of Congress, July 9, 1918, takes pleasure in presenting a Bronze Oak Leaf Cluster in lieu of a Second Award of the Distinguished Service Cross to First Lieutenant (Air Service) Samuel Kaye, Jr., United States Army Air Service, for extraordinary heroism in action while serving with 94th Aero Squadron, 1st Pursuit Group, U.S. Army Air Service, A.E.F., over the region of Montfaucon and Bantheville, France, 5 October 1918. Lieutenant Kaye encountered a formation of seven enemy machines (Fokker type). Regardless of their numerical superiority, he immediately attacked and by skillful maneuvering succeeded in separating one enemy plane from its formation and after a short combat shot it down in flames.*

On another occasion, he shot down a German Fokker armed with a new Spandau-model machine gun that was air-cooled and able to fire 650 rounds a minute. Kaye went to the crash site and recovered the machine gun so that it could be examined. His closest call came when an "air shell" shot away part of his propeller and he was forced to land.

During aerial combat, Kaye was credited with shooting down four confirmed German Fokkers and three probables. He was promoted to captain and served as the commander of the Ninety-fourth Squadron's First Flight.

At the close of the war, pilots of the Ninety-fourth painted their Spad airplanes in distinctive colors. Sam painted his light blue with red and white polka dots. He called the airplane his "Acrobatic Easter Egg." The Ninety-fourth remained in Europe for several months as the last remaining U.S. Army Air Service squadron.

Sam Kaye continued to live in Columbus after his return from France. He owned the Columbus Auto Co., which was the local Ford dealership. He died in 1939. Unable to attend the funeral because of a business commitment, Eddie Rickenbacker sent a huge floral arrangement forming the insignia of the "Hat in the Ring" Squadron.

Columbus Air Force Base was originally named Kaye Field in January 1942, but the name was changed to Columbus Army Air Field in April of that year due to confusion with the older Key Field in Meridian. Planes often flew to the wrong field, as it was spelled "Kaye" but pronounced "Coy." The names were easily confused over aircraft radios, and mail was often delivered to the wrong base.

In 2007, the auditorium at Columbus Air Force Base was named in Sam's honor. His uniform is also displayed there.

Blue Rider, a British company, sells a decal kit for plastic model Spad airplanes titled "Samuel Kaye's Easter Egg Spad XIIIC." It is the only airplane kit listed that includes an individual's name in the title.

Sam's son, John M. (Jack) Kaye, was a U.S. Army Air Corps fighter pilot in the Pacific during World War II.

Chapter 4

COLUMBUS AIR FORCE BASE

BEFORE COLUMBUS AIR FORCE BASE THERE WAS PAYNE FIELD

Several people have asked how long an air base has been here. The answer surprised most people, as Columbus Air Force Base was not the first pilot training base in the area. The first was Payne Field at West Point. Payne Field is a little-known but very historic airfield that has also been called Mississippi's first airport.

World War I brought aviation to the forefront, and the army needed bases to train pilots. In 1917, West Point, Mississippi, was selected as the site for one of those training bases. The field was constructed on 533 acres of open prairie about four miles north of town.

The field was named in honor of Captain Dewitt Payne. Captain Payne, the commander of the 182nd Aero Squadron at Kelly Field, Texas, was flying to the aid of a pilot who had crashed into the top of a tree when his plane crashed. He died on February 1, 1918, from injuries suffered in the crash.

The pilots at Payne Field trained in Curtiss JN-4 airplanes, which were called "Jennys." The Jenny had a top speed of seventy-five miles per hour and a ceiling of eleven thousand feet. The first squadron arrived on March 10, 1918. By May 1, the field was fully operational, with 125 Jennys soon in the air. People in West Point, not being accustomed to airplanes, called them "buzz wagons."

Jennys lined up at Payne Field in 1918.

Accidents were frequent, and in the first four months of operation there were four fatal plane crashes. Airplane crashes, however, were not the primary health concern. In June 1918, the surgeon general of the Public Health Service stated that Payne Field was located in "one of the worst malaria belts of the United States." Physicians there reported that 20 percent of their practice consisted of malaria cases.

Payne Field played a role in one of the milestones of aviation. The first North American transcontinental round-trip flight occurred in 1919. The flight, made by Major Theodore Macauley and his mechanic, Private Staley, began in January 1919. Macauley was flying west from Montgomery, Alabama, in a DH-4 (de Havilland) when its propeller was damaged during a rainstorm. He was able to land at Payne Field for repairs and then continued on to complete his historic trip. There was, though, a delay of over a week at Payne Field, as all of the rain had made the runway too muddy for the de Havilland to take off.

In all, some fifteen hundred pilots trained at the field during its operation. The base closed in March 1920. Shortly after it closed, the Interstate Airplane Company of Dallas, Texas, purchased much of the field. Its plan was to develop a "municipal flying field" with passenger service from the East to Shreveport, Dallas, Fort Worth and Wichita Falls. Apparently it was a plan that never materialized, as the former airfield is now thicketed agricultural land with no visible sign that it had once been a busy military base.

THE BEGINNINGS OF COLUMBUS AIR FORCE BASE

It was in the early 1930s that community leaders in the Columbus area began pursuing an air base. Captain Sam Kaye, Herman Owen and T.C. Billups were among the first to promote an air base or airport to be located at Columbus. Billups helped secure the full support of his old college friend, Congressman John Rankin, but that initial effort was unsuccessful.

As the European conflict intensified in 1940, the City of Columbus and Lowndes County approved the issuance of $30,000 in airport bonds. Then, in February 1941, citizens from Columbus and surrounding towns including Starkville, West Point, Macon and Aberdeen met to work toward securing defense-related industries. Ed Kuykendall was elected the chair of the new association.

Mississippi's congressional delegation provided its support, and Congressman Pat Harrison learned that Columbus was one of eight sites under consideration for an air base. Although unsuccessful, the earlier efforts had been remembered by the Air Corps. A local site committee, chaired by William Propst, suggested three possible locations for the air base.

In March 1941, Ralph Webb, Birney Imes and Ed Kuykendall contacted General Walter Weaver at Maxwell Field in Montgomery, Alabama, and arranged for him to come to Columbus to inspect the possible sites. General Weaver liked a site nine miles north of Columbus on Highway 45. Columbus then passed a bond issue to purchase the needed land, most of which sold for twenty-two dollars an acre.

On June 9, 1941, the War Department gave approval for the location and construction of an Air Corps base at Columbus. Congress authorized funds totaling $4,123,943 for the construction of the base. Actual construction began on July 23, 1941. Highway 45 went through the middle of the base site, so it was relocated to its present location east of the base.

Colonel Louie Mallory was the first base commander, assuming command on October 21, 1941. He served as commander until April 5, 1945. By mid-January 1942, the base was basically completed at a cost of over $7 million. On January 22, 1942, the new base was named Kaye Field after highly decorated World War I Columbus aviator Sam Kaye. Within a few days of the base being named, one thousand troops and forty-one aircraft arrived as Kaye Field was designated an advanced training school.

It was not long before a serious problem arose with the base's name. It was so similar to Key Field at Meridian that airplanes were landing at the

A 1943 postcard of Columbus Army Air Field. *Courtesy of* Commercial Dispatch.

wrong base. On April 6, 1942, the name was changed to Columbus Army Flying School, and then, on April 28, 1943, the name was again changed to Columbus Army Air Field.

During World War II, 7,412 pilots earned their wings at Columbus. The base was later used as a California Eastern Airways contract pilot training base during the Korean War and then the Strategic Air Command's 454th Bomb Wing. It's now home to the 14th Flying Training Wing. In 2008, base historian Connie Lisowski compiled and wrote an excellent 174-page illustrated history of Columbus Air Force Base.

A History of Columbus Air Force Base has now been published and is being sold by the Base Community Council. Copies may be purchased at Neel-Schaffer, Inc., located at 2310 Martin Luther King Jr. Drive in Columbus.

COLONEL "JOE DUCK" AND THE HURRICANE

Major Joseph Duckworth arrived at Columbus Army Air Field (then Kaye Field) in early 1942. He rented a Columbus antebellum home and merged not only into his work at the base but also into the social life of the town.

Lieutenant Colonel Joseph Duckworth at his desk in 1942. To his friends in Columbus he was known as "Joe Duck."

The April 1942 "Columbus Pilgrimage Guide" included the home (now known as "Magnolia Hill") as a "Star Home presently occupied by Major Joseph B. Duckworth." To the people of Columbus, he became known simply as "Joe Duck."

Little did the citizens of Columbus know the important role in aviation that Colonel Duckworth would play. That role became apparent when, in November 1942, Duckworth's efforts to improve safety and better train pilots resulted in his accomplishments being featured in *Time* magazine. His innovations in instrument instruction and flying led to his being known as the "father of Air Force instrument flying."

He is now, though, most noted for making history when he and Lieutenant Ralph O'Hair became the first pilots to admit to intentionally flying through the eye of a hurricane. Out of his flight evolved the Air Force Hurricane Hunters and the modern tracking and study of hurricanes.

During early 1942, the U.S. Army Air Force was experiencing an excessive rate of pilot training accidents and fatalities at all of its training bases. At the twin-engine advance flying school, which the army had just opened at Columbus, the base commander, Colonel Louie C. Mallory, decided to do something about the problem. He assigned his training director, Major Joseph B. Duckworth, to figure out the problem and fix it.

Many of the problems seemed to center on the twin engine A-29 Lockheed Hudson. Instructor pilots hated it and said it was "full of green dragons." It was the transition trainer to the B-26 that the combat pilots loved.

What Duckworth found was that the instructor pilots were not being properly trained to teach cadets how to fly a trainer-bomber that was "mighty hot to fledglings." Duckworth reported back to Mallory, and the qualifications to become an instructor pilot at Columbus were upgraded. Additionally, a "Flying Evaluation Board" of four officers was established to evaluate and retrain instructors. He also found a deficiency in instrument flying training and started the "full panel attitude system of instrument flying."

Between May and October 1942 the number of students at Columbus doubled, but the number of accidents decreased by 44 percent. Soon, instructor pilots from bases as far away as the Pacific Coast were sent to Columbus to be evaluated. Then, in November 1942, Major General Ralph Royce put newly promoted Lieutenant Colonel Duckworth's system in place throughout the entire fifty-six-station Southeast Training Command.

The innovative success story of Mallory and Duckworth was then featured in a November 30, 1942 *Time* magazine article titled "Teaching the Teachers."

In 1943, Lieutenant Colonel Duckworth was commander of the U.S. Army Air Forces "Instructors' School (Instrument Pilot)" at Bryan, Texas. It was there that Duckworth's most notable aerial experience occurred. On the morning of July 27, 1943, a hurricane was making landfall near Galveston, Texas. Duckworth and Lieutenant Ralph O'Hair were having breakfast with some veteran British pilots at the base. The British were kidding Duckworth because American airplanes were being removed from the storm's path, and they implied that the American planes and pilots were just not good enough. Duckworth got tired of the ribbing and decided to do what no pilot had ever admitted to intentionally doing. He and O'Hair decided to fly through the eye of the hurricane and shut up the British

They took off from Bryan Field and headed for Galveston in an AT-6 single-engine trainer. As they approached Galveston, the air traffic control tower at the Houston Airport asked them on the radio if they realized there was a hurricane at Galveston. When informed of their plans, the tower asked where to send the search parties to find their wreckage.

They completed the flight and returned to Bryan Field. Upon landing, they were met by the base's weather officer, who wanted to fly back through the storm and collect data. He climbed into the airplane, and Duckworth flew through the storm a second time. The base meteorologist made observations and kept a record of the flight The U.S. Air Corps quickly realized the value of flying into a storm to measure its intensity and provide better warnings. Within a year, regular reconnaissance flights were being made into tropical storms and hurricanes. Today, the Air Force "Hurricane Hunters" still fly into storms and are based at the Keesler AFB in Biloxi.

Colonel Duckworth retired from the U.S. Air Force in 1955 and served for a time as the head of the safety bureau of the Civil Aeronautics Board in Washington, D.C. He died in 1964 in Battle Creek, Michigan.

The significant innovations in pilot training developed by Colonel Duckworth began at Columbus Army Air Field. His legacy remains at Columbus AFB with the continued training of the world's best pilots. His memory is recalled in the Base Operations Building, which is named for him and contains a small display honoring him.

Thanks to Dave Trojan for suggesting an article on Colonel Duckworth.

Chapter 5

BLACK HISTORY

TRACING AFRICAN AMERICAN ROOTS

I am frequently asked what resources are available for local African American genealogy and history. There is actually a lot more information available than people realize. Some of the seldom-used resources include old plantation records, church registers of early white churches, legal or court documents and political broadsides and materials. These are all largely untapped sources.

Archives such as the Billups-Garth Archives at the Columbus-Lowndes Public Library and the Special Collections at the Mississippi State University Library are full of collections detailing the lives of people, black and white, who lived here during the 1800s. In Columbus, old Lowndes County legal records are found in the Billups-Garth Archives. In other area counties, those records are still at the courthouses.

The earliest legal records in this area are found in Monroe County, which was established in 1821 and originally contained all of Mississippi situated east of the Tombigbee River. One of the earliest records concerns William Cooper, a free black man working and trading along the Tombigbee River during the 1790s.

Before the Civil War, most African Americans in the South were slaves and were considered property. Because they were considered property, their names and some information about them are given on property inventories contained

A 1930s photo of the gathering at an African American family reunion in Mayhew, Mississippi.

in probate or estate records. In Lowndes County, some of the official county slave record books have survived. Pre–Civil War plantation and farm records, which can also be found in the archives, often contain lists of and information about slaves. Postwar records contain similar information about tenants.

One example is the records of the T.C. Billups and James Sykes farms in Lowndes County. Those records are located in both the libraries at Columbus and Mississippi State. They contain much slave and tenant information from the late 1840s to the 1880s. One book even lists slave births, marriages and deaths at the Billups Farm during the late 1840s and early 1850s. An 1863 Sykes letter tells of a family servant acting as a Confederate spy during the Vicksburg campaign.

Old legal records may contain not only useful genealogical information but also examples of the horrors of slavery. Lowndes County criminal files from the 1850s include cases of people being charged with felonies for the inhumane treatment of slaves—several people were even charged with murder. There is one interesting case where several prominent Columbus slave owners were sued and had to pay damages for helping another person's slave escape to freedom. There are many court cases involving the ownership or the hiring out of slaves. These cases usually provide names, ages and sometimes other family information.

Political materials, especially from the volatile Reconstruction era, are full of information about people. Often, broadsides, or single-page printed notices, were circulated and provided the names and occupations of people either for or against certain candidates or issues. While their original intent was not good, they now give very useful information. One such document (circa 1870) from Lowndes County tells how people voted in an election and gives their places of employment.

Early African American records can often be found at older white churches. For example, the following African American records are found in the parish register of St. Paul's Episcopal Church in Columbus.

Funerals:
Dick a slave of John Dixon age 35 on 30 January 1864 burial at Negro Cemetery
Nanny a servant of B.S. Green age 64 on 28 September 1864 burial at Negro Cemetery
Mary Sturdivant (Colored) [no age given] *October 1853 burial at City Cemetery*

Marriages:
Jim Evans (Colored) to Ella Baskerville (Colored) 21 October at Methodist Chapel by Rev. William Mumford
John Greenfield (Colored) Margaret Newlan (Colored) 20 November 1867 at St Paul's by JT Pickett
Mingo Kelley (Colored) to Alace Peters (Colored) 25 December 1873 at St Paul's by JL Tucker and Mrs. CC and Miss Annie Hopkins.
Ralph (Lee) slave of Mr CE Lee to Josephine (slave) of Thomas C(B). Bailey 27 September 1862 at residence of Mrs Caroline Lee by John Coleman
Phil (slave) to Virginia (slave) of Mrs Ross 15 May 1865 at residence of Mrs Ross by Bishop WM Green
Albert Vaughan (Colored) to Clarisa Halbert (Colored) 18 February 1866 at residence of Dr. Vaughan by Bishop W M Green
Lizzie [Young] *(slave) to _____ 19 February 1859 at residence of Col. Young, Waverly & by Rev. James D. Gibson.*

When researching the history of area African American families, there are a lot more resources available than most people realize. These primary sources can provide a gold mine of information.

FOLLOW THE DRINKING GOURD

Recently, there have been several television programs about the Underground Railroad—the network established in antebellum times to help escaping slaves make their way to freedom.

Did a branch of the Underground Railroad reach into our area? There were a few people in Lowndes County who were openly opposed to slavery, but there is no record of any other activities. There is, however, some musical folklore that may answer that question.

"Follow the Drinking Gourd" is an old African American spiritual that is said to be a verbal road map for slaves escaping from the Tombigbee River Valley north of Mobile. Although there is some question as to whether or not the song actually was associated with the Underground Railroad, it has, through recordings, books and tradition, become a part of the story.

There are several versions of the song—this is one of the more popular versions:

> *When the sun comes back and the first quail calls,*
> *Follow the Drinking Gourd.*
> *For the old man is waiting for to carry you to freedom,*
> *If you follow the Drinking Gourd.*

This verse seems to say that, in the spring, when the quails start to nest, it is the time to leave and to follow the drinking gourd or North Star. If you head north there will be help along the way. The key language of the other verses always ends with "follow the drinking gourd" and says:

> *The riverbank makes a very good road,*
> *The dead trees show you the way,*
> *Left foot, peg foot, traveling on.*

The banks of the Tombigbee River will be the "road," and dead trees along the riverbank will be marked with symbols of a left foot and a peg foot. One of the legends suggests that the route was marked by a man called "Peg Leg" Joe.

> *The river ends between two hills,*
> *Follow the Drinking Gourd.*
> *There's another river on the other side.*

A tintype photograph of slave "Aunt Kinzie" taken in Columbus around 1860. She was the cook for Dr. Cornelius Hardy at his North Side home now known as Magnolia Hill.

The headwaters of the Tombigbee are located in the hills of southern Tishomingo County. Across those hills, still traveling north, one finds the Tennessee River. The "road" continued north along that river.

Where the great big river meets the little river,
For the old man is awaiting to carry you to freedom if you
follow the Drinking Gourd.

In Paducah, Kentucky, the Tennessee River flows into the Ohio River. Across the Ohio River was freedom—there would be someone there to help the escaping slaves to safety.

Today, the Adventure Cycling Association promotes a 2,100-mile bicycle trail from Mobile, Alabama, to Ontario, Canada, following the route of the Underground Railroad as described in "Follow the Drinking Gourd." Among the not-to-miss historic highlights listed along the trail are two Columbus sites, the Missionary Union Baptist Church and the archives of the Columbus Library.

And yes, I have met people bicycling through Columbus following the Drinking Gourd Trail.

BLACK HISTORY AND THE COLONIAL TOMBIGBEE VALLEY

The influence of blacks in the development of the Tombigbee River Valley began with seven or eight blacks who served under Hernando de Soto during his expedition of 1539–1543. De Soto crossed the Tombigbee River in what is now the Columbus area in December 1540.

One of the most interesting figures in Mississippi's colonial history was Simon—"the Brave free Black." Simon was a free black French officer who commanded a company of forty-five black French soldiers during the Battle of Ackia (present-day Tupelo) on May 26, 1736.

The French force, which consisted of about six hundred soldiers, was dispatched to Fort Tombecbe (located on the Tombigbee River about ten miles south of Gainesville, Alabama) to prepare to attack the Chickasaw Indians and their English allies. The French force then proceeded to the mouth of Tibbee Creek, where they camped for three days, and then to a camp near present-day Amory before reaching the Chickasaw villages.

The Chickasaws, with assistance from British traders, repulsed the assault by the French and Choctaws. After the French force was soundly defeated, several soldiers questioned the courage of Simon's company.

To show his bravery, Simon ran back through the concentrated fire of the Chickasaws to the Indian village. There he threw a rope over the head of a Chickasaw horse and rode it back to the French lines through a shower of rifle fire. He was greeted with cheers, and no one ever again questioned the bravery of Simon or his company.

During the American Revolution, the closest battle to Columbus was fought at Mobile, Alabama, on March 8, 1780. There, a combined force of Spanish soldiers and Tombigbee River settlers attacked the English Fort Charlotte. The first man wounded in the assault was a free black man. Lorenzo Montero, another free black, commanded a cannon in a Spanish battery during the successful assault.

At the end of the American Revolution, England surrendered West Florida to Spain. By 1785 there were more than sixty free blacks living in the Mobile District. In 1792, the Spanish governor of West Florida wrote, "The Colored People have served during the late war with great courage and usefulness."

During the 1790s, a free black man named William Cooper was trading with the Indians living along the Tombigbee River. In 1791, Cooper was selling horses for fifteen dollars a head. The next year he was delivering corn and tobacco to a place called "the hurricane on Tom Bigby River." In 1794, Cooper worked on the construction of a fort on the Tombigbee for John Turnbull. Turnbull was an American who operated a trading business under Spanish license out of Mobile, Natchez and Baton Rouge. Cooper fell in love with Turnbull's slave servant, Medlang, and took her as his wife after trading his horse, Cooper's Grey, to Turnbull for her.

In colonial times, blacks played a very significant role in the exploration and settlement of the Tombigbee River Valley. Unfortunately, while their stories have been passed down, very few names have survived.

ANDREW JACKSON AND THE FREE MEN OF COLOR

We all know about Andrew Jackson's historic victory over the English at the Battle of New Orleans on January 8, 1815. We have also learned that Jackson's army was composed not only of U.S. Regular Army regiments but also backwoods militia and Jean Lafitte's Baratarian pirates. Actually, Jackson's army was even more diverse and represented a true cross section of the American South.

Official records show that Jackson's army was composed of the following troops: U.S. Regular Army regiments; Louisiana, Tennessee, Kentucky, Mississippi and Orleans militia; Baratarians; free men of color; and Choctaw Indians. The Choctaws were from what is now east central Mississippi and were under the command of Pierre Jugeant, who was said to be Choctaw Chief Pushmataha's nephew.

Prior to the climactic battle, the Choctaws terrorized the English camps at night while the Baratarians, under the command of Captain Dominque You, manned artillery battery No. 3. There were two battalions of free men of color—Major Lacoste's Louisiana free men of color and Captain Daquin's Santa Domingo free men of color.

While we generally relate the Battle of New Orleans with the final fighting that occurred on January 8, 1815, the initial skirmishing began on December 23, 1814. Prior to this, on December 18, General Jackson had reviewed his troops. He prepared addresses that were to be read to each unit by his aids-de-camp, Livingston and Butler. *Niles' Weekly Register*, a Baltimore newspaper, published Jackson's address to the "Men of Color" in its January 28, 1815 edition.

An 1849 engraving of the Battle of New Orleans.

To The Men of Color

Soldiers—From the shores of Mobile I collected you to arms—I invited you to share in the perils and to divide the glory of your white countrymen. I expected much from you, for I was not uninformed of those qualities which must render you so formidable to an invading foe—I knew that you could endure hunger and thirst and all the hardships of war—I knew that you loved the land of your nativity, and that, like ourselves, you had to defend all that is most dear to man—But you surpass my hopes. I have found in you, united to these qualities, that noble enthusiasm which impels to great deeds. Soldiers—The President of the United States shall be informed of your conduct on the present occasion, and the voice of the Representatives of the American nation shall applaud your valor, as your General now praises your ardor. The enemy is near; his sails cover the lakes, but the brave are united; and if he finds us contending among ourselves, it will be for the prize of valor, and fame its noblest reward.

By command   Thomas A Butler   Aid-de-Camp

The address appeared in an article titled "Events of the War." The article opened by reporting, "We are yet without definite intelligence from New Orleans. The news will probably arrive this day, that will, at least relieve our suspense." Other news included that of a peace treaty that was signed on December 24, 1814, in Ghent, Belgium, ending the war between England and the United States.

They Sang the Blues

Although I've heard blues music all my life, I paid little attention to it until I was at Ole Miss. Along with several other members of the DKE fraternity, I went to Memphis one weekend to hear a blues concert in Overton Park at "the Shell." There we saw bluesmen such as Mississippi Fred McDowell and Furry Lewis. After that, we often went to Huey's in Memphis to hear Furry play.

We contacted Furry to see if he would play for a fraternity party. He said he would and that he would only charge fifty dollars, beer to drink and a barbecue rib plate. I drove to Memphis to pick him up. It's one of those occasions when I really regret not having a tape recorder.

Driving back to Oxford, I was playing a Joan Baez folk music eight-track (I guess that dates me). She was singing "John Henry," and Furry said, "Cut that off." I asked him why, and he responded that that was not the way he had taught her to sing that song. He then complained that, while flying back from Europe, the airline had lost his guitar. I asked him what he had been doing in Europe, and he said that he had been opening for the Rolling Stones.

On another occasion, Furry told me that he had invented bottleneck blues. He said that he was the first to use a glass slide, originally using a Gilbey's Gin bottle neck. He added that nothing else had ever sounded as good.

At first I thought he was feeding me a line, but I soon found out that Furry had opened for the Rolling Stones on at least two European tours. He had also appeared in several movies, and Joni Mitchell's "Furry Sings the Blues" was written about him. He had begun playing blues in the 1920s and had played with the W.C. Handy Orchestra. There are now two Smithsonian albums with his music. The second time Furry played at a party for us, he said he was going to be recording songs for the Smithsonian the next day.

I later asked Furry why he had played for us for almost nothing. He laughed and said if he weren't doing anything else he would even play for free for people who liked his music.

Roxie's Place was a juke joint at White Station (near West Point) where Howlin' Wolf often played.

My experiences with Furry made me realize that there are also some great bluesmen from the Golden Triangle area. There was Big Joe Williams, who lived in Crawford, and Howlin' Wolf, who grew up in White Station near West Point.

Joseph Lee Williams was born in Crawford, Mississippi, in 1903. Big Joe became a legend in blues and folk music. His early career began with the Rabbit Foot Minstrels in the 1920s; then, in 1930, he recorded with the Birmingham Jug Band. In the '60s and '70s he toured Europe and Japan. He became known as the "King of the Nine-String Guitar." He died in Macon in 1982 and is buried in Crawford.

In 1979 and 1980, Michigan State University had an archaeological project along the Tombigbee River. We had a party for them in West Point and got Big Joe to come up and play. The folks from Michigan all brought their Big Joe albums to get autographed. They could not believe we could have someone so famous play for a party. Like Furry, Big Joe only charged fifty dollars to play for some local people who just liked his music.

In 1910, Howlin' Wolf was born Chester Arthur Burnett in White Station, near West Point. He is said to have been taught to play the guitar by Charley Patton. He admired Jimmy Rodgers and developed his own famous howl based on Rodgers's "blue yodel." He sang the blues locally and in the Memphis area until he was discovered by Sam Phillips, who would later discover Elvis. In the early 1950s, Wolf moved to Chicago, where he was considered one of the "classic Chicago bluesmen." He lived there until he died in 1976.

Wolf inspired some of the all-time great rock musicians. He especially influenced the Rolling Stones and Eric Clapton, who recorded albums with him in London.

Like Furry Lewis, Wolf had also played for DKE fraternity parties at Ole Miss in the 1960s.

Howlin' Wolf was inducted into the Rock and Roll Hall of Fame. His biography begins: "Howlin Wolf ranks among the most electrifying performers in blues history, as well as one of its greatest characters."

Those interested in the history of blues and its links to our area should visit the Howlin' Wolf Museum in West Point.

Chapter 6

WORLD WAR II AND COLUMBUS'S GREATEST GENERATION

STORIES TO PRESERVE

I have been blessed to grow up as a child surrounded by relatives who were veterans of not only World War II but also World War I and the Spanish-American War. Close friends have served everywhere from Korea and Vietnam to Afghanistan and Iraq. Those who have served in the military have risked and often given their lives so that this country can be free. We owe them a debt we can never repay.

History that is unrecorded is lost, and the stories and accounts of our family and friends who are veterans are a priceless heritage that cries out to be saved. One thing that we can do is record and preserve their stories.

My father was a tail gunner on a B-17 bomber during World War II. He was shot down near Frankfurt, Germany, in 1944 and spent a year as a German POW. He would talk very little about his experiences. I recall going to see the movie *The Memphis Belle* with him. He commented that the combat scenes in the movie were unbelievably accurate and that the writers must have talked to someone from his crew. Except for that and some funny stories about American airmen adjusting to life in England, he did not mention much.

Shortly after my father died, a letter appeared in the Ninety-sixth Bomb Group Historical Association newsletter. It had been written by a member of

Names and addresses of fellow POWs written on the back of Red Cross–supplied cigarette packages by Rufus Ward Sr. during World War II.

my father's squadron and described what happened when my father was shot down. That letter, along with an article in *American Ex-POW* magazine and the Ninety-sixth Bomb Group's history, told the story.

On May 12, 1944, Staff Sergeant Rufus Ward Sr. was the tail gunner on Smokey Stover Jr., a B-17 from the 337th Squadron of the 96th Bomb Group based at Snetterton Heath, England. That day near Frankfurt, Germany, the squadron was attacked by more than sixty German fighters. Smokey Stover Jr. was heavily damaged, with its left wing almost shot away and two engines set on fire.

Communications had been cut to the tail, and Ward did not hear the pilot's orders to bail out. Still firing his .50-caliber guns at a German fighter, he suddenly saw his pilot and co-pilot parachute past his window. As Ward was about to bail out, he discovered the waist gunner and the ball turret gunner lying wounded on the catwalk. He assisted each of them with their parachutes and helped them out of the aircraft before he bailed out. All survived and became prisoners of war.

Twelve of the twenty-six aircraft from Snetterton were shot down on the May 12 mission. Ten aircraft had been lost on a bombing mission on May 8. In that five-day period, the air base at Snetterton had lost half of its aircraft and crews. The life/capture expectancy of an air crewman was six missions, and my father had been on his sixth mission.

We owe our veterans a debt of gratitude that we can never repay, but that should not keep us from trying. There are many untold stories of heroism and sacrifice that need to be preserved. If we don't do it, they will be forever lost.

Remembering Those Who Served

Memorial Day is the day set aside to honor the men and women who made the supreme sacrifice to preserve our freedom. Those souls, along with all who serve and protect us, should be honored every day—not just Memorial Day and Veterans Day.

Today marks the sixty-sixth anniversary of D-Day, and it brings to mind the role that people from our area played in World War II. World War II seems like old history now, but I grew up surrounded by relatives to whom it was very real. My father, a B-17 tail gunner, was shot down over Frankfurt, Germany. He was captured and taken to Stalag Luft IV, where Dr. Julian Boggess was also held as a prisoner of war. Tom Hardy was a corsair pilot in the South Pacific. Jack Kaye was also a pilot in the Pacific. Bill McCarter was the forward fire control director for an artillery battery in Europe. Carleton Billups was a B-25 pilot in Europe. And sixty-six years ago today, Orman Kimbrough of Greenwood landed on Omaha Beach, where he knocked out a German machine gun nest that had pinned down his company, thereby earning the Silver Star.

There is a good reason that their generation has been called America's greatest. Because our community has so many who have done so much, I have only mentioned relatives whose stories made an indelible impression on me as a child.

However, there are many others who gave the greatest sacrifice and whose names are now seldom heard. Names I recall hearing include James Dickson of Aberdeen, who died when he was shot down over Germany. David Tandy and James Hollingsworth of Columbus were also killed in action. Gunter Watson died in the Italian campaign, while Howard Nolan died in a plane crash at Hatfield Heath, England. There are so many others from the recent past. They were not just lost during World War II—many were lost in Korea, Vietnam and the Middle East. We should never forget what they did, and we should always honor them for what they gave up to keep us free.

Of all the stories I recall, there may be none more poignant than that of Jesse "Red" Franks. When Pearl Harbor was attacked, Red's father was pastor of First Baptist Church in Columbus. Meanwhile, Red was studying at the Southern Baptist Theological Seminary in Kentucky. He wanted to be a minister like his father. As a theology student, Red knew he was not going to be drafted—but he also knew what his duty was, so he enlisted a few days after the attack.

A June 6, 1944 D-Day beach as viewed from a U.S. Army Air Corps Ninety-sixth Bomb Group B-17.

He became a bombardier on a B-24 in the Air Corps and went to North Africa with a Liberator Squadron. On August 1, 1943, he lost his life during an air assault on the Ploesti oil refineries in Romania. The night before the raid, he wrote home: "It will be the biggest and toughest raid yet...we will get our target at any cost...Our planes are made for high altitude bombing but this time we are going in at 50 feet above our target...I know that it will save many lives from the results, so any cost is worth it. So Dad, remember that, and the cost, whatever it may be, was not in vain."

Red's heroism and story have survived. His photograph is included in the *American Heritage History of World War II*, and his story is told in David Colley's book, *Safely Rest*.

Over the years, I have heard so many stories of unrecorded heroism and necessary but thankless jobs well done that space does not allow for all of them to be mentioned. I encourage everyone to preserve the legacy of all who have served our country by recording their stories. The Billups-Garth

Archives at the Columbus Library provide a place where such accounts can be preserved, in hopes that future generations will not forget what their parents and grandparents did for them.

THE PASSING OF THE GREATEST GENERATION

Peter Pitchlynn's 165-year-old words to his brother rang loudly this week. Pitchlynn grew up at Plymouth Bluff, his childhood marked by the Creek Indian War of 1813. He returned to the area in 1847, later recalling warriors and incidents of a wartime childhood. He concluded his letter by saying: "What brave noble fellows they were. They would have fallen and died around our little fort ere they would have allowed a Muskoke [Creek Indian] reaching us with their Tomma Hawks, among those who figured in those scenes how few are living."

My cousin Tom Hardy passed away last week. Tom epitomized what Tom Brokaw dubbed "The Greatest Generation." To me, Pitchlynn's comments are especially poignant, for when I was a child, Tom introduced me to Plymouth Bluff. His memorial service was held sixty-eight years to the day after my father's capture in Germany.

Tom was a marine pilot in the South Pacific during World War II. His medal citations read like something out of a movie. A wartime *Commercial Dispatch* article includes a photo of him receiving "3 gold stars in lieu of the 2nd, 3rd and 4th Air Medals [for] night forays against the Japanese...in the Ryukyu Islands in which he destroyed three enemy planes."

As Pitchlynn once described the heroes of his childhood, so now are the heroes of World War II. Not many are left. To that generation we owe a debt of gratitude that can never be repaid.

On one of those occasions when I really regret not having had a recorder, Tom was with my father at an air show in Starkville. At the show was a B-17, and parked nearby was an F-4 Corsair like the one Tom flew. The Corsair was complete with the checkerboard markings of Tom's squadron. I had never heard either of them talk much about their time in combat, but on that day they walked between the planes discussing and comparing experiences with Japanese and German fighter planes.

Most of the stories they told me were of the lighter moments. Tom once described how a fighter plane from his squadron was to carry an important

Left: Rufus Ward Sr. standing beside a B-17 at a Starkville air show where he and Tom Hardy traded stories. Ward, a tail gunner on a B-17 during World War II, was shot down over Frankfurt, Germany, captured and held as a POW.

Below: Tom Hardy shown standing beside his F-4 Corsair. Hardy was a marine fighter pilot in the South Pacific and was decorated for night forays in the Ryukyu Islands during which he shot down three Japanese planes.

document from their island station to Australia. He described how the machine guns and ammunition were stripped from the airplane before its mission. It seemed that the flight was a perfect opportunity to load the plane on its return flight with the rarest of wartime supplies—beer. The less weight from needless things such as guns and ammo, the more beer that could be carried on the long flight. Tom said that the risk of encountering an enemy fighter was replaced by the thought of cold beer on a hot Pacific island. The flight was a success, and upon returning, the beer was buried in the sand on the beach. Aviation fuel was then poured over it, and the rapid evaporation of the fuel quickly cooled the beer.

My father told of the time his crew had a weekend pass to London. They went barhopping the first night but were constantly dogged and threatened by a military policeman (MP) with possible disciplinary action. The next night, they went to dine at one of the better restaurants in London. Just after they were seated, a waiter came over and told them that an MP wanted to buy them a drink. They laughed, commenting that their antagonist from the night before must be feeling guilty, and replied with, "No thanks." The waiter returned and said the MP would like to pay for their meal—they again said, "No thanks." Then, the waiter returned and told them that the MP wanted them to join him at his table. Thinking that the MP from the night before had a real guilt trip going, they replied that they "wanted nothing to do with a !*#* MP." The waiter left with an ashen face and then returned saying the Member of Parliament was most distressed. My father said they quickly left the restaurant.

At the Starkville air show, the conversation between Tom and my father had been nothing to laugh about. They discussed the difference in living and dying at twenty thousand feet and friends who never came home. That great generation is passing all too quickly. It was only a couple of months ago that Jack Kaye, another South Pacific campaign pilot and hero, left us—and now Tom.

To veterans who are gone, and to those who remain, we owe an unpayable debt. But sadly, as for those of World War II, the words of 165 years ago ring all too true today: "What brave noble fellows they were...among those who figured in those scenes how few are living."

ROMMEL'S AFRIKA KORPS WAS JUST
DOWN THE ROAD

Aliceville, Alabama, was the site of one of the largest POW camps in the United States during World War II. Construction of Camp Aliceville began in August 1942, and the first prisoner of war arrived in June 1943.

Those first prisoners of war were all Germans captured in North Africa. Many of them had been members of General Erwin Rommel's famed Afrika Korps. They arrived in Aliceville on trains, carried by the Frisco Railroad. As the war progressed, German prisoners from all over Europe were sent to Aliceville.

The camp grew to contain over four hundred buildings and house 6,100 prisoners of war. It also employed over 1,000 military and civilian guards and personnel. The camp was a barbed-wire compound complete with guard towers. Across its four hundred acres were barracks, bakeries, chapels, theaters, a hospital and other assorted buildings. There were sports fields, gardens and even an amphitheater.

Camp Aliceville had a reputation for humane treatment of prisoners of war. That caused resentment among some local residents. At a time when Americans were experiencing the rationing of food and other items, the Germans at Camp Aliceville were receiving ample meals with fresh meat and vegetables. The camp also had an orchestra and theater productions— some prisoners even played soccer. Noted puppeteer Walter Buettner, who was drafted into the German military and later captured at Normandy, was even allowed to form a puppet theater at the camp.

There was a legitimate reason for the good treatment the prisoners at Aliceville received. The American military hoped that this treatment would be reciprocated to American prisoners of war in Germany. In fact, until January 1945, Germany did treat Allied prisoners of war far better than did Japan. However, in January 1945, as Russian troops moved into Germany, thousands of poorly clothed and underfed American and Allied prisoners of war were forced to march over five hundred miles in freezing weather for three months.

Camp Aliceville closed on September 30, 1945, and all that remains at its former site is a stone chimney next to an industrial park. However, the camp lives on at the Aliceville Museum.

In recent years, the memory of the good treatment the German prisoners received has paid remarkable dividends. After learning of the creation of the

Aliceville Museum, former German prisoners of war and their families have donated sketches, paintings, woodcarvings and other memorabilia to the museum. They have also given German uniforms worn by former prisoners at the camp.

The German donations, along with donations from local residents, have resulted in the museum featuring the largest World War II German prisoner of war camp exhibit in the United States. The Aliceville Museum is located at 104 Broad Street NE in downtown Aliceville—about a thirty-minute drive from Columbus. It is open Monday through Friday from 10:00 a.m. to 4:00 p.m.

NINETY-FIVE YEARS OF RED CROSS SERVICE

Recently, Mayors Robert Smith of Columbus and Scott Ross of West Point signed proclamations designating March as Red Cross Month. For ninety-five years, the Red Cross has played an important role in helping people in the Golden Triangle area. It was in 1917 that the local chapters were founded in response to the events of World War I.

During World War I, the Red Cross assisted local servicemen and their families, helped provide needed personal articles for soldiers and, in 1918, opened an office at Payne Field in West Point. The local chapters became inactive after the war ended and the need to assist servicemen decreased.

As World War II broke out in Europe and Asia, the local chapters were reactivated. The chapters provided help ranging from assisting servicemen's families with emergencies to knitting olive drab sweaters for soldiers. The Red Cross also opened an office at Columbus Army Air Field in 1942.

By February 1945, the Lowndes County chapter had raised $38,072 for national programs, loaned over $10,000 to local service families with emergency needs, rendered 9,487 service contacts and assisted seven hundred families with disaster relief. In addition to providing assistance, the chapter held regular parties at the air base. It was during World War II that the local chapter also became more involved in disaster relief.

Many people along the Tombigbee River associate the Red Cross with relief efforts during the formerly frequent winter and spring floods. During World War II, two floods along the Tombigbee found an active Red Cross chapter ready to help. In 1946, the Lowndes County chapter acquired four

A photo of the Lowndes County Chapter of the American Red Cross taken in 1917 at the First United Methodist Church in Columbus. *Beginning front row left to right*: Sue Mae Lincoln, Rachel Newby, Mrs. T.O. Burris, Mrs. Robert Mann and Mrs. J.M. Flynn. *Others pictured left to right are*: Mrs. W.H. Brooks, Mrs. Louise Landrum, Mrs. John T. Stanford, Mrs. S.B. Street (Captain), Mrs. Louise Wood Cox, Mrs. Henry G. Cox, Mrs. Will Richards, Miss Fannie Worthington, Mrs. W.B. Harrington, Mrs. W.F. Patty, Mrs. J. Rupert Richards, Mrs. Parker Reeves, Mrs. T.O. Burris Jr., Mrs. W.R. McKinley, Rosa Locke, Mrs. W.C. Watson, Mrs. Annie L. McGeorge, Mrs. J.T. Searcy, Mrs. R.E. Johnston, Mrs. Waights G. Ottley, Mrs. Henry M. Beard, Mary Lou Frazee, Mrs. Will E. Frazee, Mrs. W.H. Simpson, Mrs. T.J. Locke Jr. and Mrs. H.F. Simrall.

surplus assault boats to use in flood relief. Since then, whether the disaster has been a fire, a flood or a tornado, the Red Cross has responded.

My father always credited the Red Cross with helping him survive World War II. A 1946 *Commercial Dispatch* article reported on his speaking about the yearly Red Cross fund drive:

> *Rufus Ward, former staff sergeant in the Air Corps and tail gunner of a B-17, who was shot down over Germany and held prisoner for nearly a year, said in his talk that "dollars and cents could not pay for what the Red Cross had meant*

to him during his entire period of service." In the States as well as overseas the Red Cross was on the spot when needed most. During his imprisonment at Stalag Luft 4 in Germany the POW's received as many packages (Red Cross) as transportation would allow and the packages meant not only food but hope as well. When he was liberated and sent to France he received supplementary feeding from the Red Cross, which provided orange juice and malted milks to rebuild his prison-starved body. A Mississippi Red Cross Canteen worker (Dorothy Stout of Vicksburg) wrote a letter telling of his liberation to relieve the mind of his anxious family even before they were notified by the government.

In late April 1945, Dorothy Stout and two other Red Cross workers were on a German road in a "clubmobile" near the front lines. They were providing coffee, doughnuts and cigarettes to soldiers. On April 28, they encountered fifteen hundred Americans newly liberated from a German prison camp. Among the former POWs was Ward, with whom Stout had mutual friends in Mississippi. She wrote a letter that day to Mae Puckett in Columbus and described him as dressed "in various parts of Jerry [German] uniforms" and having "quite long hair" and a "sort of Robinson Crusoe" appearance.

In a September 23, 1995 interview in the *Jackson Clarion Ledger*, Stout recalled that day and said, "We rushed up to them amid their shouts of 'No, no, you're going to get full of our lice. If you touch us you'll have to get deloused.' But nothing stopped our joyous, thankful hugs and greetings...It was without a doubt the most delightful and memorable moment of World War II for me.'"

Today, the Red Cross continues to help service personnel and their families in times of need. Though the local chapters were merged into a single regional chapter last year, Red Cross offices are still located in both Columbus and Starkville, and services have not changed. The local advisory board continues to ensure that, with community support, the Red Cross will always be there when help is needed. However, we must always remember that it is our support of the Red Cross that makes this possible.

Chapter 7

CHOCTAWS AND CHICKASAWS

PUSHMATAHA

It was a glorious sun-filled day, with beautiful flowers covering a wide plain. Among the few trees was a giant centuries-old red oak that shadowed an immense area. Although it had survived many centuries unscathed, the oak still had not accomplished the purpose for which the Great Spirit had planted it.

It was noon when a great black angry cloud rose in the west and, in an appalling uproar fringed with lightning, whirled across the plain. With a shattering crash a frightful tornado swept a devastating course. When the sun returned, the great oak was but oddly shaped splinters scattered across the plain.

Not a vestige of the tree remained, but the purpose of its creation was fulfilled, for standing in its place—equipped and ready for battle—was Pushmataha. Thus did Pushmataha describe his birth.

Pushmataha, or Apushimataha, was probably the greatest leader of the Choctaw Nation. He was born in 1764 in a log cabin on the banks of the Noxubee River near present-day Macon. Little is known about his parents or early life. As a young man, he distinguished himself in battle with Osage Indians west of the Mississippi River and the Creek Indians in what is now west Alabama. He was given the name Pushmataha, which probably means "one whose tomahawk is fatal in war or hunting."

McKenney and Hall's 1842 portrait of Pushmataha. The portrait was based on Charles Byrd King's 1824 portrait that had been painted in Washington.

Gideon Lincecum knew Pushmataha and described him as being "about five feet ten inches in height" and having "that inexplicable attribute about him which belongs only to the truly great, that which forced the ejaculation, 'who is that?' from all observant strangers."

The Choctaw Nation was divided into three districts, and Pushmataha became the chief of the Southern District around 1805. He remained chief until his death in 1824. He was famous for his oratory—especially that at a great council in 1811. There, the noted Shawnee leader Tecumseh attempted to get the Choctaws to join his Indian confederation. Pushmataha spoke of his friendship with the "Virginians"(Pushmataha often referred to white Americans as Virginians) and convinced the Choctaws to reject Tecumseh's alliance as one that would only lead to war and disaster.

In the Creek Indian War, the Choctaw Nation, at Pushmataha's urging, allied with the United States and Andrew Jackson. Pushmataha was commissioned a lieutenant colonel in the U.S. Army but given the uniform of a general. He led Choctaw warriors to assist Generals Jackson and Claiborne in fighting the Creeks. Under Pushmataha, the Choctaws attacked the Creek village at the falls of the Warrior River (Tuscaloosa) and joined with American forces at the Battle of the Holy Ground and the capture of Pensacola.

Pushmataha always said that "his hands were white," meaning he had never killed an American but had killed many enemies of America. He is said to have fought in twenty-four battles.

He died on December 24, 1824, when he came down with pneumonia while leading a Choctaw delegation in Washington. He was buried in the Congressional Cemetery with full military honors. His funeral procession consisted of over two thousand people, including companies of the U.S. Marine Corps, U.S. Volunteers, congressmen and Andrew Jackson. His last request was that "the big guns" be fired over his grave—and they were.

What Indian Tribe Lived Here?

Frequently, someone will show me an arrowhead they have found and ask whether it is from the Choctaw or the Chickasaw Indians. I get funny looks when I tell them neither and that it's not even an arrowhead. To make matters worse, I usually add that the Indians around here did not live in tepees either.

The easy part of this to explain is that most of the artifacts that are called arrowheads are actually knives or small spear points. What people commonly call bird points are the true arrow points. In the Tombigbee area, prehistoric Indian houses were generally made of wood with cane-braced walls covered in mud and had thatched roofs. By the early 1800s, many Choctaws and Chickasaws were living in log houses. Several of the wealthy tribal leaders were even living in two-story frame houses. They were a far cry from the tepees shown on television and in Westerns.

What is not very clear, though, is the early development of the Indian tribes in the Tombigbee Valley. Archaeologists have divided the pre-history of this area into periods of similar artifacts or cultural remains.

The first Americans were called the Paleo-Indians. They were nomadic hunters who arrived here over fourteen thousand years ago. They hunted with spears, and their most noted type of spear points were called Clovis points. The Paleo-Indian Period was followed by the Archaic Period about ten thousand years ago.

An 1837 reprint of a 1591 engraving by Theodore de Bry depicting an Indian village in
what is now the southeastern United States.

The Archaic Period is subdivided into the Early, Middle and Late
periods. About three thousand years ago, Indians in the Tombigbee
Valley began making pottery during what is called the Woodland Period.
They also constructed rounded-top burial mounds. That culture was
followed by the Mississippian Period about one thousand years ago.
These people developed chiefdoms, or city-states, and constructed
large flattop temple mounds.

It was during the disintegration of the chiefdoms, at the end of the
Mississippian Period in the 1400s, that we began to see the formation of
today's Indian tribes. The period of early European contact is called the
Proto-historic Period and runs from about 1500 to 1700. There are only a
few written cultural records from that time. It is from the Historic Period,
or post-1700, that extensive cultural records of Native Americans in the
Tombigbee Valley have survived.

When De Soto arrived at the Tombigbee River in December 1540, he
first encountered the Chickasaw Indians just west of the river—probably in
Lowndes, Okitbbeha or Clay County. To the south were the early Choctaw.
To the west were the Chakchiumas, and in northwest Clay or eastern
Chickasaw County were the Alabama. The Choctaws and Chickasaws

were in their formational stages during the 1500s and were assimilating the smaller tribes in the area.

The Choctaws were slowly moving north, as were the Chickasaws, and by the early 1700s Tibbee Creek was recognized as the dividing line between the two tribes. The land where Columbus is located was ceded by the Choctaw Treaty of Fort St. Stephens in 1816. Amory (south of Gaines Trace) was in the Chickasaw cession of 1816. Starkville and Macon are found on lands ceded by the Choctaw Treaty of Dancing Rabbit Creek in 1830. West Point and Aberdeen are located on land acquired through the Chickasaw Treaty of Pontotoc in 1832.

The Indians who lived in our region were a far more cultured and refined people than is commonly realized. A good example of this are the broken pieces of fine English dinnerware found on many Choctaw and Chickasaw house sites. The Indians enjoyed European items as much as the early Euro-American settlers. These are not the artifacts that most people expect to find on Indian sites.

Playing Ball 181 Years Ago

Ballgames have been a part of Native American culture since prehistoric times. Early French missionaries found the Choctaw playing a form of stickball in 1729. Stickball in various forms was popular among almost all Indians in eastern North America. It was from stickball that the modern game of lacrosse evolved.

In the 1800s, the Choctaw form of the game was played on a field of anywhere from one hundred to five hundred yards in length but with no designated width. At each end a post would be set up. The object was to use ball sticks to throw the ball (made from deer hide) and hit the post. Ball sticks were two to two and a half feet long with a loop pocket at one end to catch and throw the ball. The ball could not be touched by anyone's hands.

The ballgames were used for both entertainment and settling disputes. Games between different communities could have thousands of spectators and hundreds of players. Depending on the circumstances of the game, each team could have from twenty to over two hundred players. Generally, ten to twenty points was set as the winning score, with a point scored each time a team struck its post with the ball.

An 1867 engraving from a George Catlin painting of an 1839 Choctaw ballgame.

In 1829, Columbus resident Gideon Lincecum decided to gather together some of the best Choctaw ballplayers and take them on a tour of the eastern United States. Lincecum planned to take two teams of twenty players each to put on exhibitions of Choctaw stickball. With assistance from John Pitchlynn, word was sent out for interested Choctaw ballplayers to gather at Oak Slush Creek (a few miles west of Columbus) on November 28, 1829.

By noon on November 28, over four hundred Choctaw ballplayers had assembled. There was to be a lottery for the selection of the ballplayers who would make up the two traveling teams. To ensure he got the forty best players, only the names of those preselected players were placed in the hat from which the drawing was made.

On the morning of November 29, 1829, Lincecum and the forty Choctaw ballplayers set out on what would be an eight-month tour of stickball exhibitions. They soon crossed the Tombigbee at Tanyard Creek (now called Moores Creek) and entered Columbus via Military Road. One wonders if perhaps they commenced their journey by playing an exhibition game in Columbus.

Not far from the old Tombigbee River crossing and Tanyard/Moores Creek stands an ancient cypress tree. Had the Choctaws played an exhibition game, the tree would have marked the edge of the most likely location for a ball field; thus the site of the first ballgame in Columbus.

Columbus's new soccer complex is linked by location with the rich 181-year multicultural heritage of ball playing in this area—a heritage that is still overseen by an ancient cypress sentinel.

Chapter 8

ART, LIBATIONS AND MUSIC

THE ART OF HISTORY

When researching southern history, it is always interesting to find first-person accounts of earlier times; it's even more fascinating to find early images. It is surprising just how many of those early images are around and how they relate to the present.

Many of the flowers that we see today in local gardens were first pictured in Curtis's *Botanical Magazine*. It was established in England by William Curtis in 1787 and contained hand-colored engravings of plants and flowers with descriptive articles about each. It is still published today as *Curtis's Botanical Magazine* by the Royal Botanic Gardens, Kew.

One 1804 illustration in particular comes to mind—that of the oakleaf hydrangea, which was first recorded in south Alabama around 1780. In 1791, William Bartram published a book with what is probably the first illustration of the oakleaf hydrangea. As a child growing up in Columbus, I can remember going with my grandmother to dig up wild specimens to transplant to our yard.

During the 1770s, William Bartram traveled across the lower South, observing and sometimes drawing its people and landscape. In the late 1780s he begin writing a book on his travels. *Travels Through North & South Carolina, Georgia, East & West Florida, the Cherokee Country...* was published with some of Bartram's illustrations in 1791. It is still considered a classic account of

An 1867 engraving of a circa 1840 portrait of Peter Pitchlynn by George Catlin.

the natural history of the early American South. It is still in print and often simply called *Bartram's Travels*.

From the earliest European exploration of North America, many artists have sketched or painted their views of Native American people. Probably the most vivid images were watercolors by John White, who sailed with Sir Walter Raleigh to Roanoke Island in 1585. During the early 1590s, Theodore de Bry turned those watercolors, along with paintings by Jacques le Moyne, into what became widely published engravings. De Batz, during the 1730s, and Du Pratz, between 1718 and 1754, provided illustrations of the Choctaws and the Natchez Indians. Other artists also attempted to visualize the New World. Unfortunately, many of the early artists gave European attributes to both the southern landscapes and peoples.

Between 1820 and 1830, Charles Bird King painted portraits of notable Native Americans. The portraits were placed in the Indian Gallery of the Smithsonian Institution in Washington. The gallery burned in 1865, and most of the portraits were lost. One portrait that has survived (in private hands) is that of Pushmataha, the great Choctaw chief. Though most of the originals were lost, Thomas McKinney and James Hall had published

120 of King's paintings as lithographs between 1838 and 1842. In doing so they have preserved many historic images that otherwise would have been forever lost.

The most prolific painter of early American scenes was George Catlin. From 1830 to about 1860, Catlin painted hundreds of American and Native American scenes. Among his portraits were images of Choctaws, including Ha-tchoo-tuc-knee (Peter Pitchlynn) and Mo-sho-la-tub-be, who lived in what are now Lowndes and Noxubee Counties respectively. Another interesting painting was that of the "White Sand Bluffs, on Santa Rosa Island," which is a view of the Gulf beach near Pensacola. Catlin's book, *Manners, Customs, and Conditions of the North American Indians,* can still be found in print and contains about three hundred illustrations.

When thinking of historic images, most people do not think of John J. Audubon, but his illustrations do not only contain birds or animals. Audubon wanted to paint his subjects in their natural habitat, so although his birds are interesting, it is often the background that catches my attention. Those backgrounds provide beautiful illustrations of the flora and landscape of the South during the 1820s. One southern plant that figures prominently in Audubon's art is the oakleaf hydrangea, which seems to have been a popular image among early artists.

The development of photography in the mid-1800s resulted in untold numbers of photographs of people and places. Also, mid-1800s billheads often contained engravings of the storefront or types of merchandise offered. The widespread introduction of illustrated magazines in the second quarter of the nineteenth century also provided a wealth of images. Archives such as the Billups-Garth Archives at the Columbus-Lowndes Public Library, Special Collections at the Mississippi State University Library and the Mississippi Department of Archives and History are filled with photographs and other images of local interest.

Southern history and art are deeply intertwined, and to fully study one requires an understanding of the other.

NICOLA MARSCHALL'S COLUMBUS PORTRAITS

Nicola Marschall was a Prussian-born portrait painter whose works included portraits of Abraham Lincoln, Jefferson Davis, Otto Von Bismarck and

Marschall's 1875 portrait
of Ida Sykes Billups in her
wedding gown.

many other notable figures of the mid-to late 1800s. Marschall studied art at
the Dusseldorf Academy and immigrated to the United States in 1849. He
settled in Mobile but soon moved to Marion, where be became noted as a
portrait painter.

During the Civil War, he is credited with designing the Confederate
"Stars and Bars" flag and the Confederate army uniform. The gray of the
Confederate uniform came from the color of Prussian army uniforms.

After the war ended, the depressed economy of the South forced
Marschall to travel to different towns and cities to paint portraits and
finally to move to Louisville, Kentucky. In 1870, Nathan B. Forrest, then
president of the Selma, Marion and Memphis Railroad, wrote a letter of
introduction on behalf of Marschall to A.S. Humphries, S.M. Meek and
John M. Billups of Columbus. Forrest recommended Marschall as a skilled
painter of portraits. Probably as a result of that letter, Marschall came to
Columbus during the mid-1870s and spent several months painting portraits.

Marschall painted a large number of portraits while in Columbus. For the
Billups family alone he painted at least nine, one of which was that of Ida
Sykes Billups. T.C. Billups and Ida Sykes were married on January 28, 1875,
and Marschall painted a portrait of her in her wedding gown. The portrait
was completed that April in Louisville, Kentucky. It was shipped to Columbus

on May 1 after having been exhibited in Louisville for a week. Marschall charged $150 for the portrait, $50 for the frame and $2 for shipping.

Marschall had a studio in Louisville and acquired a national reputation for his work. Examples of his portraits were exhibited at the 1876 Centennial Exhibition in Philadelphia, where he won a medal for his work. He continued painting until 1908 and died in Louisville in 1917.

Many homes in Columbus are still graced with family portraits that he painted.

AND THE BAND PLAYED "GARY OWEN"

Civil War reenactment bands are noted for their playing of period music. Bands re-creating southern units are always thought of as playing "Dixie" and "The Bonnie Blue Flag," but the popular music of the South was much more varied.

I have an old vinyl record that appears to be from the 1960s and is titled *Band Music of the Confederacy*, *"Making History Live," Volume 4, the 1st Brigade Band Recreates the Historic 11th Mississippi Regimental Band, CSA, a Presentation of Heritage Military Music Foundation, Inc.*

The Eleventh Mississippi Regiment was one of the more noted Confederate army units and was composed of many area soldiers. Company A was the University Grays from Ole Miss. The Prairie Guards of Company E were from Lowndes County and served under the command of Henry Halbert. The Prairie Rifles (Company C) and the Chickasaw Guards (Company H) were from Chickasaw County and included many soldiers from the West Point area. Company F, the Noxubee Rifles, was under the command of Thomas Stokes of Noxubee County. Stephen Moore commanded Company I, the Van Dorn Reserves of Monroe County.

Several songs on the record are stated to be arrangements composed for the Eleventh Mississippi Band based on popular songs of the day. They were found in the Eleventh's songbook, which was in possession of "the late Walter A. Holloway, a renowned Civil War collector." Those songs were: "Come Dearest the Daylight Is Gone," "Gary Owen," "My Maryland," "Juanita" and "Sweet Home."

The record jacket states that the band participated in a concert with other bands (both Confederate and Union) during a pause in

The Eleventh Mississippi Regiment in Virginia during the fall of 1861 as pictured in an 1861 edition of the *London Illustrated News*.

the Fredericksburg Campaign during the winter of 1863. The band of the Eleventh Mississippi was "said by many to be the best in the Rebel Army."

In one of those strange coincidences of history, "Gary Owen" (the song associated with General Custer's Seventh Cavalry and its massacre at the Battle of the Little Big Horn and the charge of the Light Brigade) may well have been the music played by the band of the Eleventh Mississippi Regiment before Pickett's charge at Gettysburg. The Eleventh suffered 340 casualties out of 394 soldiers.

I once suggested that, because of its association with the University Grays, "Gary Owen" would be a historically accurate substitute for "Dixie" at Ole Miss football games. It was quickly pointed out that "no it wasn't, as military units that had played it in the past had usually gotten slaughtered."

The Joints and Honky-tonks of Old 82 West

Establishments serving strong libations and good food have a long history around Columbus. From the rye whiskey of Lincecum's and Pitchlynn's 1820 storehouse to the fried catfish that gave its name to the one hundred block of Fourth Street, the mixture of food and beverages has been with us since the founding of Columbus. As a matter of fact, the first tavern in Columbus predated the first church building by almost ten years.

It was west of the Tombigbee, though, that the glory days of local joints reached their height. Their beginnings are associated with the earliest names in Columbus history. The first tavern license in Columbus was located in William Cocke's house, which was located where the Tennessee Williams home now sits. But that may not have been the first local watering hole—that distinction belongs to a location on the west bank of the Tombigbee River in what was then the Choctaw Nation. It was there, around 1819, that Gideon Lincecum and John Pitchlynn Jr. entered into a partnership to operate a storehouse and tavern at the Columbus Ferry crossing. This was also the final location of Bob's Place, giving over 170 years of social continuity to taverns on the west bank of the river. It was there that the first classic Columbus tavern story took place.

Gideon Lincecum told of an occasion when a Choctaw (who was also a good customer) came in and decided to play a joke on him. Gideon told him that he had a new drink he wanted him to try. He then mixed him a cocktail that was half rye whiskey and half cayenne pepper. The Choctaw killed it in one swallow and remained composed, though beads of sweat began breaking out across his brow. He then politely excused himself and went into a back room. Gideon then heard a piercing scream followed by deathly silence. Just as Gideon worried that he had overdone the joke, the Indian emerged as though nothing was wrong. He walked back to the bar and said, "Best drink I've ever had. Give me another one just like it." And so began the first of many stories about Columbus joints, dives and honky-tonks.

During Prohibition and the decades that followed, the law did not crimp the style of those who wanted a drink. Establishments selling alcoholic beverages thrived west of the river. They ranged in flavor from the Jungle to the Silver Spur. The Jungle was built during the early 1940s and was a real honky-tonk. The Silver Spur was located down the Old Macon Road. It looked like a large barn but was famous for its good steaks and availability of good beverages. It was sold around 1970 and acquired a more honky-tonk atmosphere.

Nighttime in 1982 at the Crossroads on old Highway 82 between Columbus and Starkville.

The Southernaire was the quintessential southern beer joint. Located just past Bob's Place west of the Tombigbee Bridge, it often featured music by Big Ben and the Nomads and attracted students from Starkville to Tuscaloosa. Several years ago I was working on a case with an attorney from one of the larger law firms in Atlanta. When I told him I was from West Point, Mississippi, he asked, "Where is that in relation to the Southernaire Club?" The popularity or notoriety of the "Aire" was spread far and wide.

Each establishment had its own personality. When I think of joints west of the river, I can't help but remember Mack's Western Supper Club at Crawford. There was the Snow White, just down old Highway 82 from the Southernaire. It was a good place to get a beer inside or a fifth of liquor around back. The High Hat and the Lakeside were across the road from each other. Both were said to be rough. Another one of the old joints was called the Round House and had a sawdust floor. Fresh floors were obtained when needed from the nearby Bruce Lumber Company. The Dew Drop Inn, with its dirt or sawdust floors, was "guaranteed to have a fight going on." At the Old West Point Road and Highway 82 was the Straight Eight Jr. In the 1970s, Rasputin's and Granny's catered to the so-called hippie crowd near where the Magnolia Speedway now is. When you were hungry you went to Bob's or, if you needed that late-night cup of strong coffee, to the Coffee Cup.

At Mayhew were the Mississippi State watering holes of the Crossroads, Len Lews, the Landing and Echoles. There is the one story of the Mississippi State student from Clarksdale, whose parents noticed all his checks made out to Len Lews. They told him that they needed to speak to him about all the checks he was writing. He breathed a sigh of relief when they said that they were so pleased that he was spending all of his money on Chinese food and not wasting it at beer joints.

Across from Bob's and the Southernaire was the Coffee Cup. It was open late, and many a not-so-steady person went there to drink coffee and sober up before hitting the road. In *The Noblest Roman*, a novel about bootlegging in Mississippi by Pulitzer Prize–winning author David Halberstram, the Coffee Cup was where the bootleggers went after making their run.

No place retains the fond memories of so many as does Bob's Place. Bob's was one of those rare places that crossed generational lines. The beer was cold, the food (especially the barbecue) was unsurpassed and "Aunt Barbara" ruled from behind the counter. BooBoo served the food and kept everyone in line. James only had one arm, but to this day I have yet to find his equal for fixing barbecues, hamburgers and fries.

The tearing down of Bob's Place (for the new Tombigbee Bridge) in 1991 marked the end of an era that began at that same spot some 173 years before. George Dyson, a friend who remembers the hangouts of the fifties and sixties, once reflected: "It was the glory time in this country, Rufus. There will ne'er be another period like that…There were some bad times and bad folk, but they were far outnumbered by those who were the best of the best. It would suit me just fine if Heaven is much like the 50s…Course I have got to get there first!"

Eudora Welty's Whitehall Mint Julep

Whitehall, an antebellum home in Columbus, Mississippi, has long been known for its hospitality. Built by James Walton Harris in 1843, it was long the home of the related Harris, Hardy and Billups families. The home's basement served as a hospital during the Civil War. During World War II the basement was again used, this time as a servicemen's hangout for Columbus Army Air Field personnel. Its walls were graced with original Walt Disney Studio production art and autographed "Happy Landings at Whitehall — Walt Disney."

The guests who have been entertained there range from Confederate generals to novelist and social activist Upton Sinclair. Photographs taken

An 1850s coin silver goblet that was used to serve mint juleps at Whitehall. *Photo courtesy of Aaron Hoffman.*

at the home have appeared in publications such as *Life* magazine and the *London Illustrated News*.

Whitehall is now the home of Joe and Carol Boggess, who have lovingly restored it and continued its tradition of hospitality. In the 1950s, Joe's parents, Dr. and Mrs. Jullian Boggess, purchased the home from the Hardy family.

It is not for its hospitality, however, for which Whitehall has been nationally heralded. It is for that quintessential southern beverage: the mint julep. The recipe for the "Whitehall Mint Julep" can be found in many books and collections of southern recipes, including John T. Edge's *A Gracious Plenty*. It was even included in a May 2010 article found in *USA Today*.

The Whitehall Mint Julep recipe first appeared in print in an interview by Eudora Welty with Mrs. Billups (Lenore Hardy) in 1939. In the fall of 1939 Welty came to Columbus as part of an Associated Press travel writers' tour. The first Columbus pilgrimage was to be held the following spring, and Mrs. Billups, a pilgrimage founder and chairman, was helping host the tour. The writers were entertained at Whitehall, where they were served the Whitehall Mint Julep.

Eudora Welty then interviewed Mrs. Billups about the drink. The story of that mint julep circulated nationwide, making newspapers such as the December 26, 1939 edition of the *Detroit Times*. Interestingly, Welty wrote under the name of "Prudence Penny."

According to Welty, "A collection of recipes from the old South is no more complete than the old south itself without that magic ingredient, the mint julep. In the fine old city of Columbus, in the northeastern part of the state, hospitality for many years is said to have reached its height in Whitehall the home of Mr. and Mrs. T.C. Billups. 'The drink is refreshing,' says Mrs. Billups, needlessly enough, 'and carries with it all of the charm of the old south when life was less strenuous than it is today; when brave men and beautiful women loved and laughed and danced the hours away, but in their serious moments which were many, aspired to develop minds and souls that made them among the finest people this old world has known.'"

Lenore Billups was my grandmother, and when she heard that I was going to attend Ole Miss she said, "If you are going to the University, then you must know the proper way to make a mint julep." She was a graduate of Newcomb College in New Orleans, but my grandfather was an Ole Miss graduate. The recipe she gave me was identical to the Whitehall Mint Julep recipe she had given Eudora Welty in 1939—with one exception. That exception was that she told Welty that the proper way to serve a mint julep was in a "silver goblet thoroughly chilled," and she told me simply to use a julep cup.

The old Whitehall Mint Julep recipe is as follows:

> *Dissolve sugar in water. Bruise a mint leaf in a tablespoon of the sugar water then remove the leaf. Fill the silver goblet with crushed ice and add the tablespoon of mint and sugar water. Fill the julep cup with good bourbon (I use Old Rip Van Winkle). Put in a sprig of mint and let stand until the goblet is frosted. Then "serve rapidly."*

As Eudora Welty said in conclusion, "Who could ask for anything more?"

As Good As a First-Class Restaurant in Paris

The 1840s and 1850s were the golden age of steamboats in the Mobile trade on the Tombigbee River. When examining the cultural history of those steamboats, one of the most interesting facets is the diversity and quality of the foods served on board.

It is amazing to think that, on what was then the American southwestern frontier, meals comparable to those served in present-day restaurants could

The cabin tables of a steamboat set for a meal around 1900.

be found. It was with good reason that the steamboats of the time were called "floating palaces." The deck passengers or economy class had to provide their own food, but the cabin or first-class passengers traveled in relative luxury.

Many people even chose the steamboat they would travel on based on the boat's cook or bartender. Their importance was shown by the fact that other than the captain, pilot and clerk, the cook and bartender were usually among the highest-paid crew members. Even slave cooks and bartenders were very well treated and were not questioned on their work.

In 1858, a writer for *Harper's New Monthly Magazine* traveled on the steamboat *Henry J. King* on the Alabama River (that steamer also ran on the

Tombigbee). He compared the food and service on the Mobile-bound boat to that of a "first class restaurant of Paris."

The table set for an evening meal on the steamboat *Norma* (traveling from Columbus to Aberdeen) in 1844 was described as: "A table, extending half the length of the gentleman's cabin, groaned with the rich array of viands, fruits, and cakes...oysters and wine were prominent on the table."

An actual listing of food, beverages and condiments served on the steamboats is provided in an 1837 accounting of provisions for the Columbus-Mobile trade steamboat *Tropic*. Meats that were served included: ham, pork, beef, dried beef, beef tongue, codfish, salmon and mackerel. There were also items such as potatoes, rice, beans, and onions. There were even cheeses and assorted fruits and nuts such as figs, dried apples, preserves and almonds. Available condiments and seasonings included: mustard, catsup, cayenne pepper sauce, vinegar, salt, pepper, sugar and pickles. Beverages served included tea, coffee, French cordial (a brandy and fruit liquor) and whiskey.

Oysters were served in cooler weather. Croaker sacks of oysters were brought upriver from Mobile to Columbus by the steamboats. They became so popular that the city began using the growing piles of oyster shells to fill potholes in the streets.

The food and service provided to first-class passengers on many Tombigbee steamboats of the mid-1800s would rival any restaurant in Columbus today.

PIRATES, PIGS AND 470 YEARS OF BARBECUE

People in the Black Prairie have always taken pride in their history—and in their barbecue. Very few, though, realize how closely history and barbecue are tied.

Barbecue, or bar-b-que, is derived from a Spanish term for meat roasted over an open fire. The Spanish term *barbacoa* is said to have originated in the Caribbean and was derived from a word for the cooking practices of Indians there.

The Spanish heritage of southern barbecue runs deep. In December 1540 Spanish explorer Hernando de Soto crossed the Tombigbee River in the Columbus area. De Soto had with his expedition over three hundred hogs that were used for a supplemental food supply. The expedition's dining on roasted pork near the Tombigbee would have been the first recorded pork

A 1706 Dutch engraving depicting "Ferdinand de Soto's Cruelties in Florida." It illustrates hands of Native Americans (Chickasaws) being cut off as punishment for stealing and eating Spanish pigs. It is probably the earliest illustration of the northeast Mississippi area.

barbecue in what is now Mississippi. That also meant barbecued pork was probably the first Christmas dinner served here.

It was in 1697 that we see the first use of the word "barbecue" in English. That was by William Dampier, an English buccaneer. The word "buccaneer" was initially used in referring to Europeans who dried and smoked fish over a fire in the manner of the Caribbean Indians. Since many of those were French or English pirates preserving meat for their voyages, "buccaneer" became another word for "pirate."

The earliest local usage of "barbecue" that I have seen is in an 1825 copy of the *Virginia House-Wife* that has been passed down in the Billups family in Columbus. It contains the following:

To Barbecue Shote
This is the name given in the southern states to a fat young hog, which, when the head and feet are taken off, and it is cut into four quarters, will weigh six pounds per quarter. Take a fore quarter, make several incisions between the ribs, and stuff it with rich forcemeat; put it in a pan with a pint of water, two cloves of garlic, pepper, salt, two gills of red wine, and two

of mushroom catsup. Bake it and thicken the gravy with butter and brown flour; it must be jointed and the ribs cut across before it is cooked, or it can not be carved well, lay it in the dish with the ribs uppermost; if it be not sufficiently brown, add a little burnt sugar to the gravy.

A more recent recipe for southern barbecue sauce was recorded by Eudora Welty around 1939. She told of Aberdeen's famous barbecue parties given by James Acker at his home, the Magnolias. According to Welty, his barbecue sauce recipe was as follows: "Heat together: 4 ounces vinegar, 14 ounces catsup, 3 ounces Worcestershire sauce, the juice of 1 lemon, 2 tablespoons salt, red and black pepper to taste and 4 ounces butter. Baste the meat constantly while cooking."

Many believe that the southern barbecue tradition reaches its height at Magowah, a prairie gun club that began in 1906. Their old sauce recipe contained more than fifteen ingredients and was prepared in a cast-iron kettle over an open fire. They still continue their tradition of skeet shooting and barbecuing both pork and lamb there. The club's 1940 recipe is:

Barbecue Sauce serves 100

1 pound of chopped onion;
4 pounds of fat, bacon or ham, melted;
2 quarts of vinegar;
1 quart of water;
1 pint of mustard, prepared;
1½ quarts catsup;
4 ounces sugar, brown;
salt;
red pepper;
chili powder (optional)
Worcestershire sauce, (optional) 2 ounces.

Fry onions in melted fat until tender and slightly brown. Add remaining ingredients; mix thoroughly.

Our region has been, and still is, blessed with a number of unbelievably good barbecue establishments and stands. Three especially good ones that are no longer with us come to my mind—Bob's and Sugg's restaurants in Columbus and Roosevelt's Brame Avenue BBQ stand in West Point.

Chapter 9

CIVIL WAR

"No Personal Antagonism"

It was late February 1864, and fighting had been occurring all around West Point, Mississippi. Union General William "Sooy" Smith had led seven thousand troops from Memphis into Mississippi to lay waste to the Mobile and Ohio Railroad and Confederate supply depots, including the huge supply complex at Columbus. By February 20 his soldiers were in West Point.

His goal was to link up with General William T. Sherman near Meridian after having destroyed the railroad and Confederate supplies from Okolona to Meridian. In the process Smith would also burn private homes and barns. The strip of the Black Prairie from south of Tupelo to Macon was called the "breadbasket of the Confederacy" because of its great corn production. Smith intended to eliminate it as a source of Confederate supplies.

As Smith moved his troops into West Point, Confederate General N.B. Forrest was gathering his forces along Sakatonchee Creek near the Ellis Bridge three miles west of town. Forrest had also dispatched Colonel Tyree Bell to protect the Waverly Crossing on the Tombigbee River, General Gholson to Hulka Creek Bottom between West Point and Houston and Colonel Jeffery Forrest to Tibbee Creek Bottom. The Sixth Mississippi Cavalry was ordered to protect the Tombigbee crossing at Cotton Gin Port (near Amory) but was diverted to Judge Calvert's farm on the Houston Road to scout Sakatonchee Creek in case General Smith tried to outflank Forrest's men at Ellis Bridge.

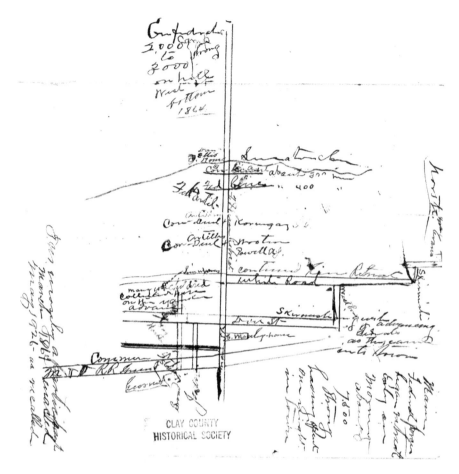

Diagram of the Battle of West Point drawn by T.M. Mosely, a Confederate soldier who participated in the battle. *Courtesy of Bryan Public Library in West Point, Mississippi.*

General Forrest's scattered troops covered all the important river and creek crossings around West Point but totaled fewer than six thousand men. However, General S.D. Lee was quickly coming up from the south to reinforce him.

Smith became worried that he might be trapped in West Point with Confederate forces on three sides. He then made an unsuccessful assault on the Confederate lines at Ellis Bridge. At about the same time, he began withdrawing his troops back north toward Okolona. There would be skirmishing all the way to Okolona, where a larger battle would later be fought.

While all of this was going on, both sides had scouts out attempting to determine the enemy's movements. Many of the Union troops were retreating up North Division Street in West Point. Along a fencerow near North Division Street, in the area where a TVA substation is now located, one of those odd events of war occurred.

John Young of the Confederate Eighth Mississippi Cavalry Regiment (who was from this area) had been sent to scout the Union troop movements. He hid behind a fence near North Division Street in order to survey the landscape. He slowly rose up to look over the fence. Unknown to him, a Union soldier from the Second Iowa Cavalry Regiment, William Rooker, was concealed on the other side of the fence. Both rose up at the same time to take a look around. Young and Rooker found themselves looking "eyeball to eyeball" at each other.

Totally startled and not knowing what to do, they simply shook hands and introduced themselves. They then began talking. Rooker stated, "If God lets me live through this war, when it is over I am coming back. It's the prettiest place I have seen." They then decided that as they had "no personal antagonism" they would each withdraw peacefully.

Rooker survived the war, and he did move to West Point. He bought a farm just north of town near where he had encountered a Confederate soldier along a fence. Shortly after arriving in town he attended Sunday services at the First Christian Church. There he found John Young, the former Confederate soldier. They became close friends after having shared a unique wartime experience.

In a final twist, Rooker's daughter, Amy, ended up marrying Young's son, James. James later became mayor of West Point. He and Amy had a daughter, Vira, who married David Calvert.

Sometimes a true story is better than any fiction.

The local history room at the Bryan Public Library in West Point contains many transcriptions of letters describing the fighting there in 1864 and the experiences of the townspeople.

FORTRESS COLUMBUS

Recently I underwent major heart surgery at Baptist Hospital in Columbus. While the surgery could not have gone any better and the doctors, nurses and staff could not have been any more caring, I am an outdoors person who, for four days, could only look out of a window in the critical care unit.

As I looked out, I could not help but recall Adair Cox. Mr. Adair, as I called him, was a civil engineer and close friend of my parents. During the early 1960s he was heavily involved in the survey and engineering of what would be first Lowndes General Hospital and eventually Baptist Hospital. He knew my interest in history and was always good about calling me if he came across something he thought I might find interesting.

As I lay in the CCU, I recalled once walking over what became the site of the hospital with Mr. Adair. He was showing me a Confederate Civil War entrenchment he had discovered. Most of the entrenchment is now lost to neighborhood, hospital and school development. Portions of the entrenchments may yet survive in the shallow ditches between the hospital and Heritage Academy.

Few people realize the extent of the fortifications that once surrounded Columbus. The construction of fortifications commenced in June 1862; by August 14, 1863, it was completed. Columbus was then completely encircled by either entrenchments or rivers. Major concentrations of Confederate troops were stationed one and a half miles north of town on both the Aberdeen Road and the Military Road.

Historian Gary Lancaster (I consider him the authority on Columbus's Civil War history) has found in the "Official Records" of the Civil War a fascinating document. On October 1, 1863, Union Major General S.A. Hurlbut forwarded to the U.S. XVI Corps the report of a "scout" sent down the M&O Railroad. The scout had visited Columbus and described the situation there.

> At Columbus, Miss., are also two batteries, Rice's and Thrall's, with 120 men, & Columbus has been fortified with 20-odd miles of earth-works and…It would take about 50,000 men to occupy these fortifications—a small number could not do any good. Engineer Low, who fortified the place, said "it was thought it may be of use to General Bragg in the future." The town is situated on the east side of Tombigbee River. The river is bridged with a very long bridge. Near the bridge is a small stockade, which can hardly keep 20 men in—a dash of 100 cavalrymen, can take it. The river can be forded at Main Street, but this ford is fortified with ditches and earth-works. But there is a ford 3 miles below the town, which is not well fortified, and they could not stop the crossing of cavalry as well as in town. But the best place to cross the Tombigbee River is between Cotton Gin and Aberdeen, Miss. In Columbus can be found several millions of Government goods, as Maj. W.J. Anderson has (at the arsenal building)

one of the largest army clothing factories in the Confederacy, and plenty of every other article usually found in the quartermasters department.

All the above-mentioned places are under the command of Brig. Gen. Dan. Ruggles who will not fight, but run. If our cavalry makes a raid on the Memphis and Ohio Railroad, and passes through Columbus, they should get hold of a man by name of Griesem, in William Cady's livery stable; also a n____ man named Guss, at Cady's Hotel. The above named men are well acquainted with the roads and fords in the States of Mississippi and Alabama, as they have been stage and wagon drivers most of their lives. Close to Columbus lives a gentleman by the name of George Field, who is and has been thoroughly loyal to the old Union, and would do most anything to break up the rebellion; he could give information about the Confederates' movements. Mr. Young, in that neighborhood, has 150,000 bushels of corn.

Even while lying in a hospital bed in Columbus, one still cannot escape being encircled by our area's rich history.

"Number 27 and the Pumpkin Pie"

Columbus was a major military hospital center during the Civil War. That was not a status that Columbus sought. However, its location on a branch of the Mobile and Ohio Railroad and the handling of wounded after the Battle of Shiloh in April 1862 resulted in the development of Columbus as a Confederate hospital center.

After the fighting at Shiloh, a flood of wounded soldiers arrived in Columbus on the railroad. Carolyn Burns Kaye found an account written by Reverend James Lyon that detailed the horrific scene at the Columbus railroad depot after the Battle of Shiloh. He described there being over 3,300 wounded soldiers "stacked like cord wood" around the depot. Large buildings such as the then unfinished Gilmer hotel were turned into hospitals. Even private homes were opened to receive and care for wounded soldiers.

One such home was Whitehall, the South Side residence of James and Martha Harris. In the basement of Whitehall, holes were drilled into the brick walls so that one end of a stretcher could be inserted into the wall while the other end would be propped up on blocks. There, and also at

The basement of Whitehall, the home of Mrs. James W. Harris, was used to care for wounded soldiers during the Civil War. A photo of the home taken during the 1940 Columbus Pilgrimage. *Courtesy of Billups-Garth Archives, Columbus-Lowndes Public Library.*

main hospital sites such as the Gilmer, Mrs. Harris helped care for the wounded. A white ironstone pitcher with which she gave water to wounded soldiers has been passed down in her family and, though cracked, survives to this day.

One of the most fascinating accounts of Mrs. Harris's actions was not passed down in her family but recorded in a Chicago newspaper. Not long after the death of Mrs. Harris in October 1896 a newspaper article titled "Number 27 and the Pumpkin Pie" appeared in the *Chicago Times-Herald*. It began:

"The recent death of the venerable and beloved Mrs. James W. Harris of Columbus, Miss., recalls an amusing yet pathetic hospital experience of that lady's. The women of Columbus, when necessity arose, organized a Soldier's Relief association of which Mrs. Harris was president." That organization was dedicated to "ministering to the wants of Confederate soldiers as far as lay within their power, and of nursing the sick and wounded."

Every day, Mrs. Harris and the other ladies of the association went to the hospitals and shared with the wounded their meager supplies of food and assisted in providing nursing care. One day, Mrs. Harris came upon a "young Yankee soldier" whom the doctors said was dying of typhoid fever. The attending doctor told her not to waste her time on the "poor devil of a yankee," as there was nothing more that could be done for him and he would soon die.

In a scene that would be repeated by other Columbus ladies at the origin of Memorial Day, Mrs. Harris thought of her sons in the Confederate army and wondered what would happen to them in such a situation.

She then, with "her eyes filled with tears," turned to the doctor and said, "I'm going to take that poor boy in my own special charge, and as there is any food or medicine left he shall have his share of it. And I know you well enough, doctor, to feel sure that you will expend on that yankee boy of mine as much care and skill as if he was one of my own double-dyed rebel sons."

Even with the loving care of Mrs. Harris and the attention of the doctor, the young soldier's condition grew ever more grave. Finally one afternoon the doctor said the poor boy would not survive the night. As the boy drifted in and out of delirium, Mrs. Harris asked him if there was anything she could do for him. He weakly whispered "pumpkin pie." Not knowing exactly what he meant, she asked again. The boy whispered again "pumpkin pie" and drifted into exhausted sleep.

Mrs. Harris went and baked a pumpkin pie for the boy and took it to him that evening. The next morning she went back, expecting to learn of his death. When she arrived and asked the doctor about his condition, she was told the boy had eaten the whole pie and was, by some miracle, better and asking for more pumpkin pie. With Mrs. Harris's care and more pumpkin pies, the young soldier recovered.

The Chicago newspaper article concluded, "So the boy from Maine got well, and he always declared that if it had not been for those pumpkin pies he surely must have died!" It was signed L.H. and identifiable only as a Union army veteran of the Civil War who had served as a nineteen-year-old backwoods boy from Maine.

MEMORIAL DAY AND THE LEGACY OF
DR. WILLIAM SYKES

The death of Dr. William E. Sykes and the love of his family played a major role in the origins of Memorial Day. Many articles have been written about Memorial Day and the ladies of Columbus, who were the first in the nation to honor the graves of both Union and Confederate soldiers with flowers. However, in those accounts you do not find the name of William E. Sykes.

William E. Sykes was born in Decatur, Alabama, in 1835. He was the son of George and Mary Sykes, who had moved to Decatur from Virginia. The family moved to Aberdeen in 1849. Education was important to the family, and after an extensive primary education, William attended the University of Virginia.

He then entered medical school at the University of Pennsylvania, from where he graduated in 1855. He returned to Aberdeen and opened his medical practice. Then, in 1858, he left the medical field after being given a plantation in Tallahatchie County by his father. In 1860 he married Augusta Murdock of Columbus.

When the Civil War broke out in 1861, he joined the Confederate army as a surgeon. Being behind the lines was not Sykes's nature. After about six weeks, he resigned his commission and enlisted as a private in Captain Abert's company of cavalry. His brother, Columbus Sykes, wrote that William told him "he would never shield himself behind a sick man's couch." In May 1862 he transferred to the Forty-third Mississippi Infantry Regiment as a first lieutenant and adjutant.

In October 1864, the Forty-third Mississippi was facing Union troops advancing on Decatur, Alabama. As a battle erupted on October 26, Lieutenant Sykes was in the forefront of the action. Early in the fighting Sykes was struck in the abdomen by the shell from a ten-pound Parrott gun (cannon). His brother rushed to his side, and William was carried into Decatur, where he was laid on a couch in the house in which he had been born. William's brother later wrote, "Though suffering excruciating agony, he calmly surveyed his wound and pronounced it inevitably mortal."

As he lay dying, he asked that an ambrotype (photograph) he had of his wife, Augusta, be buried with him. He directed that his last words be told to his son, James Murdock Sykes. William whispered with his last breath, "Tell Murdock never to use profane language, drink, chew or smoke tobacco, or visit improper places." Dr. William E. Sykes died at ten o'clock on the

An unidentified Confederate lieutenant whose photo was taken by a Paducah, Kentucky photographer. It was found in an 1800s album of Harris/Hardy family photos from Lowndes County, Mississippi.

morning of October 27, 1864. His body was carried back to Columbus, where he was buried in Friendship Cemetery.

William's brother, Columbus Sykes, had accompanied William's remains to Columbus and attended the funeral. After William's funeral, Columbus Sykes took a furlough so that he could visit his family in Aberdeen. He left Aberdeen around December 19, 1864, to rejoin his company. He caught up with them on December 31. On the afternoon of January 5, 1865, they made camp, and Colonel Sykes picked a spot under a tall dead tree. During the night the tree fell on Sykes and two other soldiers, killing them. His dying words were: "Tell my dear wife and children I loved them to the end." He died on January 6 and was buried in Aberdeen.

During the spring of 1866, Columbus ladies Miss Matt Morton, Mrs. J.T. Fontaine and Mrs. Green T. Hill had been caring for the graves of over 1,260 Confederate soldiers buried in Columbus's Friendship Cemetery. Their actions resulted in a desire for a formal ceremony to lay flowers on the graves of the soldiers. One of the ladies who helped organize the event was Augusta Sykes, the widow of Dr. William Sykes. As the widow of a

Confederate soldier, Augusta was able to do something—at a time when hard feelings still remained—that no one else could have done.

Augusta Sykes felt that the graves of forty Union soldiers who were also buried in the cemetery should also be decorated with flowers. She thought of the Union soldiers as husbands, fathers and brothers—just like the Confederate soldiers. As a widow, she knew the pain of the nation and took a huge step toward healing its deep wounds. Her suggestion was taken to heart, and the ladies of Columbus were the first in the nation to lay flowers on and honor the dead of friends and former foes alike.

Their action attracted national attention, and articles reporting the healing act appeared in several northern papers, including the *New York Tribune*. That article inspired New York judge Francis Miles Finch to write the celebrated poem "The Blue and the Gray," which inspired the whole country and for many years was closely associated with Memorial Day.

The sad death of a doctor-turned-soldier in 1864, and his brother in 1865, led to a brave widow taking a major step in healing a nation's deep wounds.

A FIRSTHAND ACCOUNT OF GRIERSON'S CAVALRY RAID OF 1863

One of the most famous cavalry exploits of the Civil War was the Union cavalry raid through Mississippi led by Colonel B.H. Grierson in 1863. The raid has been the subject of several books and even a John Wayne movie, *The Horse Soldiers*.

The *New York Times* apparently had a reporter imbedded within the troops. Its May 18, 1863 edition published a "Detailed Narrative" that provided a daily account of the raid by its correspondent.

The unnamed correspondent reported that he was with the Seventh Illinois Cavalry under Colonel Edward Prince at LaGrange, Tennessee, when, at 10:00 a.m. on April 17, Colonel Grierson ordered them to proceed south on the Ripley, Mississippi Road. The regiment traveled south through Ripley, New Albany and Pontotoc with only minor skirmishing.

On April 20, the Seventh continued moving south and passed around Houston. It camped that night at Clear Springs. On the morning of the twenty-first, the Second Iowa Regiment, which had been traveling with the Seventh Illinois, was ordered to "proceed toward Columbus and destroy the

A Civil War–era drawing of Union cavalry.

Mobile and Ohio Railroad as much as possible." Through a daylong rain, the Seventh continued traveling south and passed through Starkville, finally making a wet camp eight miles south of town.

At daylight on the twenty-second, Captain Forbes, with Company C of the Seventh, was detached to proceed to Macon and destroy the Mobile and Ohio Railroad there. Before proceeding on to "the little village of Louisville," Grierson's remaining force burned a Confederate shoe manufactory near Starkville. The paper's correspondent reported that Grierson "succeeded in destroying several thousand pairs of boots and shoes, also hats and a large quantity of leather; besides capturing a Quartermaster from Port Hudson."

The raid continued on through Mississippi, with the Seventh Illinois arriving "triumphantly" in Baton Rouge on May 2.

The full story of the raid and the exploits of all of the different military units involved make fascinating reading. This is especially true as much of the story takes place in our own backyard. The most readable account is Dee Brown's *Grierson's Raid: A Cavalry Adventure of the Civil War.*

Grierson himself was a very interesting figure. He was a former music teacher who did not care for horses. He also treated the local civilians far better than did General Sherman. While he destroyed railroads, telegraph lines and materials that could be used by the Confederacy, he did try to avoid the destruction of personal property. His respect for civilian property is clearly shown by an old Columbus tradition. At the close of the war his troops were said to be occupying Columbus. Some of his soldiers stole mules from the Cedars on Military Road. Grierson personally returned the mules to the home, making a most favorable impression on a former foe.

GENERAL GRANT'S COLUMBUS PLOY

History is like a big puzzle. There are scattered pieces tucked away in different collections, archives and books just waiting to be assembled. Sometimes these scattered pieces come together, helping to form a complete story.

After coming across a letter written by General U.S. Grant, an old story of a local event took on a completely new light. The letter can be found in the Alfred Whital Collection of Lincolniana at the Library of Congress. It was written by General Grant from his Vicksburg headquarters on October 8, 1863, to General S.A. Hurlburt.

Within the letter, Grant wrote: "I am just sending out all the forces that can be sent from here to drive the enemy from Canton and Jackson, with instructions to remain at Canton a few days and scout with the Cavalry as far Eastward as possible. Columbus Miss. is a point of vast importance to the enemy and if threatened would necessarily cause the enemy to detain a large force at that point. The cavalry will try to create the impression that they are going there."

Grant saw threats to the massive Confederate manufacturing facilities and the Columbus supply depot as an effective means to tie up Confederate troops defending Columbus, thereby opening up other important Confederate centers for attack. On several occasions Union troops threatened Columbus while larger forces attacked elsewhere. One such victim of that strategy was the railroad hub of Meridian, Mississippi, which was attacked and burned by General Sherman in February 1864.

When I found Grant's letter, I forwarded it to fellow local historians Gary Lancaster and Carolyn Burns Kaye. Gary responded with his research showing that Sherman had used diversions against Columbus when attacking other points. Carolyn reminded me of a local story that had been recorded in *War Memories*, a small book published by the S.D. Lee Chapter of the United Daughters of the Confederacy.

The story was titled "The Yankees Are Coming" and was written by Georgia P. Young, who was living at Waverly during the Civil War. In her recollections of wartime she wrote:

> *One glorious sunlit crisp morning in October 1863, a servant rushed breathlessly to me, exclaiming as she came, "Old Master says get ready, the Yankees are coming"...I rallied my fast ebbing courage and...gave orders to nurse and housemaid to quickly dress the children in two full suits of new clothing. This expedient was resorted to that my little ones should have a change of garments should our house be despoiled and burned, as others had been, and we turned adrift without the necessities of life... While the children were being dressed, I busied myself in packing a trunk with silver, plate and other valuables. This was my only hope of saving such things from the rapacious fingers of our expected visitors. The trunk was put in charge of a trusted slave who in my own childhood had given me many a ride on his brawny shoulder, and who, I felt sure, would do all in his power to shield me from harm. My confidence was not misplaced and sometime afterwards the trunk was brought back with its contents intact. The Federal raiding party never reached Waverly. We subsequently learned that it was in a half mile of us when they concluded they had advanced far enough for their safety, and our anxiety for a time was relieved.*

The Union cavalry party that approached Waverly, just across the Tombigbee from Columbus, occurred in the same month that General Grant had ordered a diversionary raid be made toward Columbus—thus bringing two pieces of a puzzle together.

Chapter 10

A Miscellany of History

The Crawford Panic

At nine o'clock on the morning of October 8, 1924, an almost two-and-a-half-city-block-long silver airship passed over Columbus. Traveling at fifty-five miles per hour and at an altitude of about two thousand feet, it angled slightly southwest and then west toward Greenville. After a few minutes it passed low over Crawford. It was the USS *Shenandoah,* making the first transcontinental flight by an airship. It was a brief passage that has been lost to local history.

It is always interesting to view a historic event from two different perspectives. That is especially true when those events had a local element and a slice of comedy. So it is with the USS *Shenandoah.*

The story of the USS *Shenandoah* itself is a fascinating story of the beginnings of air travel. Built by the U.S. Navy on the pattern of the great German Zeppelins of World War I, it was 682 feet long with a width of 78 feet, 9 inches and a height of 93 feet, 2 inches. As the navy's first rigid airship, it was christened and commissioned on August 20, 1923.

However, its life was short. On September 2, 1925, the *Shenandoah* was scheduled to leave Lakehurst Naval Station on a training flight to Dearborn, Michigan. Its commanding officer, Lieutenant Commander Zachary Lansdowne, requested permission to delay the flight because of bad weather. His request was denied, and it departed as scheduled. The

A 1924 U.S. Navy photo of the USS *Shenandoah* moored to the USS *Patoka*.

next morning it passed through a severe thunderstorm over Ohio and broke apart in turbulence. Of its forty-three officers and crew, fourteen (including LCDR Lansdowne) were lost when it crashed near Marietta, Ohio.

Army Colonel Billy Mitchell's public criticism of the navy's handling of the *Shenandoah* and LCDR Lansdowne's weather concerns helped lead to Mitchell's 1925 court-martial for insubordination. That court-martial ended the career of Mitchell, who is considered the "Father of the U.S. Air Force."

Our story, though, is the story of the *Shenandoah*'s historic flight across North America. It is a story that made national headlines. Although not mentioning its nearby passing, the *West Point Leader* newspaper had a lengthy article detailing the flight with the headline "Continent Spanned by the *Shenandoah*." The Columbus papers from that week are missing from both the *Dispatch* and Columbus Library archives, so the Columbus coverage is not known.

The January 1925 issue of the *National Geographic* contained a forty-seven-page account of the flight. Included was a map showing the key cities that the *Shenandoah* passed over. The route across the Deep South took it over Spartanburg, South Carolina; Atlanta and Carrollton, Georgia; Birmingham, Alabama; Columbus and Greenville, Mississippi; Bastrop and Shreveport, Louisiana; and then to Dallas and Fort Worth, Texas.

Included in the *National Geographic* article were descriptions of the cities and countryside seen during the flight. The *Shenandoah* left from the naval station at Lakehurst, New Jersey, on October 7, 1924, at 10:00 a.m. At 7:15

a.m. on October 8, it approached Birmingham and there "the mantle of smoke from her steel mills was visible." Between Birmingham and Columbus "the forest seemed without a break." It passed over Columbus at 9:00 a.m. and Greenville at 11:47 a.m.

As the *Shenandoah* passed Columbus and crossed over "the land of cotton," the scene below was one of white fields of cotton and square white bales stacked at railroad depots. Through trees and in clearings were seen dirt roads leading to "weather-beaten houses." The airship seemed to terrify chickens and livestock, and children looked up "in awe." Some of the children were seen waving in greeting, and one man was observed running into his house and coming back out waving a white tablecloth. The observer felt he was waving a greeting to the *Shenandoah*. A story from Crawford causes one to wonder if it was a symbol of greetings or actually an improvised white flag of surrender.

I had not heard the story of the *Shenandoah* passing over Lowndes County until it was mentioned to me by Tommy Gentry. Tommy remembers hearing this story and others from his father. "He loved aviation and used to tell me stories of the time that a dirigible flew over Crawford when he was a lad. The dirigible was flying at about two hundred feet in altitude in a southwesterly direction. He told me that he, my uncle William Albert Gentry Jr. (Dub) and Neil (Cornelius) Ervin were standing on the steps of the old Crawford Post Office on that day. He indicated that the direction in which she was traveling would have put it passing over the Saunders Carson Plantation. I asked if he heard the sounds of the engines and he said that he did not. He said the townspeople in Crawford 'thought the world was coming to an end.'"

Tom Hardy's father, Harris, knew of the *Shenandoah*'s coming and had Tom (then a small child) out in their front yard to watch the great airship's passing. Tom remembers watching it with fascination, recalling that when it passed to the south of his house at about one thousand feet high "it looked like it was a quarter mile long."

As is often the case when one views a historic event, whether it incites terror or inspires curiosity usually comes down to perspective.

Columbus's Five Most Interesting Buildings

I am frequently asked, "What is the oldest house in Columbus?" However, I decided to turn that around into what is the most interesting building in

The Ole Homestead, a circa 1827 vernacular raised cottage, is probably the oldest surviving house within the original 1821 town limits of Columbus. It has been approved for Mississippi Landmark status.

Columbus. When it comes to the architectural history of Columbus, I have two friends who are the experts and who I normally rely on for the best information. Here in Columbus, I usually just call Sam Kaye, but with such a potentially loaded question for a local resident I thought it best to go out of town.

For over thirty years Ken P'Pool has been with the Mississippi Department of Archives and History and has been Mississippi's go-to person in historic preservation. He first ran the department's Historic Preservation Columbus field office before moving to Jackson, where he is the longtime head of the department's historic preservation division.

I asked Ken what he considered to be the five most interesting, but not necessarily the most historically important, buildings in Columbus. Ken was gracious and brave enough to respond with his view of Columbus's five most interesting buildings.

The first he mentioned was the Williams-Gass House at the corner of Second Avenue North and Fourth Street. It was built around 1843 by Isaac and Thomas Williams, who were "free men of color." Though African American, the brothers had prospered in Columbus during the 1840s. The house is a raised cottage with a brick basement and frame principal floor. Its broad, low gable roof is typical of Carolina Lowcountry architecture, as the Williamses were from South Carolina. The Williamses moved from Columbus in 1851, and in 1858, Adam Gass bought the house from the "Estate of Thomas Williams, F.M.C." Gass then added the east wing onto the house.

Ken next mentioned the Ole Homestead at the corner of College and Third Street South. The Ole Homestead is a vernacular raised cottage that was purchased or constructed by Charles Abert around 1827. It originally faced the Tombigbee River. H.S. Bennett, who was renting it in 1830, was its first documented occupant. He later represented Mississippi in Congress. The house was enlarged and reoriented to face College Street in 1835 by John Kirk. It may be the third-oldest surviving raised cottage in Mississippi and is probably the oldest surviving house within the original 1821 town limits of Columbus. Ken finds it reminiscent of "Madame John's Legacy," an eighteenth-century house in New Orleans. The house has been approved for Mississippi Landmark status.

Of the many churches in Columbus, it is the Annunciation Catholic Church that Ken views as most interesting. The church was designed by French-born priest and architect Father Jean Baptist Mouton in a Gothic style that was inspired by Paris's thirteenth-century Church of Sainte-Chapelle. The cornerstone was laid on May 4, 1863. "The facade of the church is an eclectic assortment of French Gothic motifs. Its three-bay composition is a typically French ploy that dates to the earliest Gothic cathedrals," says Ken. The vaulted ceilings and interior plan of the church also closely duplicate the interior forms of Sainte-Chapelle. Each of the interior columns and piers is painted to appear to be marble. The church is an example of a type of Gothic form rarely found in the South and is a Mississippi Landmark.

The W.N. Puckett House on the MUW campus is considered by Ken to be one of the finest examples of a brick Queen Anne–style house surviving in the state. It was constructed on College Street around 1902 by the Columbus contracting and brickmaking firm of Lindamood & Puckett. The house exhibits one of the best examples of the beautiful and unique salmon-colored brick that was produced by Lindamood & Puckett during the late nineteenth and early twentieth centuries. That firm is still in business as the Columbus Brick Company. In 1928 the house was moved a half a block south so that Whitfield Auditorium could be built on College Street. The Puckett House is a Mississippi Landmark.

Ken could not decide between two adjacent buildings as to which he considered the other most interesting building in Columbus. One is the one-story Greek Revival building across from the courthouse that Roger Larson used for the Columbus Packet office. It had been built in the early 1840s as a law office. The other building is the three-story brick office building next door. It was constructed in a simplified Greek Revival style during the late 1850s. For many years it was the Woodmen of the World building, with its lodge hall on the third floor. The offices in the Woodmen's Building and others along "Lawyers' Row" were originally sold much like condominium offices are sold today. The building is one of the largest antebellum office buildings surviving in Mississippi.

Each of us has our own favorite building in town, so it is enlightening to see what a leading out-of-town historic preservation expert finds most interesting.

THE "W": 165 YEARS OF QUALITY WOMEN'S EDUCATION

Many Mississippi University for Women alumni will read the above title and say, "But the centennial wasn't that long ago." Well, it wasn't, but it was. If that seems confusing, it really isn't. MUW opened as the Industrial Institute and College in 1885. However, it was not a completely new school, as it evolved out of the 1847 Columbus Female Institute, which closed in 1884 so that it could be transferred to the state and reopened as a state "girls' college" the next year. That would make the "W" a year older than Ole Miss.

Although the W does not claim back to the Columbus Female Institute, there is a strong case that it could. Auburn University in Alabama claims its beginnings go back to East Alabama Male College, a Methodist school established in 1856. That is a precedent that the W could follow with the older Columbus Female Institute, as its buildings and grounds became the new school.

One day, Sam Kaye and I were sitting around discussing the little-recognized role of the Columbus Female Institute in the origins of the W. The Columbus Female Institute was established under the initiative of Colonel A.A. Kincannon on May 15, 1847, and its constitution approved a week later. Its charter was approved by the state legislature on March 4, 1848.

I have heard the comment that the Columbus Female Institute was not a real college. The school actually had both a preparatory department

A view of the Industrial Institute and College published nationally in the July 4, 1885 edition of *Frank Leslie's Illustrated Newspaper*.

and a collegiate department. The belief that it was not a real college does not stand up to a look at the curriculum put in place by the school's board of trustees. Its minutes reflect that the following courses of study were required for students in the collegiate area: "reading, analysis, penmanship, analytical orthography, arithmetic, geography, history, English grammar, composition, Latin, Greek, botany, algebra, rhetoric, geometry, trigonometry, muorology, zoology, natural philosophy, intellectual philosophy, moral philosophy, evidence of Christianity, logic, chemistry, physiology, bookkeeping, and English Literature." That was at the time a college and not a preparatory curriculum.

The interest by the trustees in making the school a state women's college was not a sudden venture. It parallels the push for better women's educational opportunities in Mississippi. In 1856 Sallie Renau began a drive to improve women's education and began working toward the establishment of a state female college. She was not successful, but she laid the groundwork for future efforts. Annie Peyton assumed a leading role in the cause and, after years of struggle, finally got a positive response from the legislature.

On June 17, 1872, the trustees of the Columbus Female Institute met with Chancellor Lyon of the University of Mississippi and decided to offer their campus as the female division of the State University. However, the legislature failed to act on the offer. Mindful of its role, the Female Institute rejected a suggestion to offer its campus to the proposed A&M College (Miss State) in 1878.

On March 12, 1884, the efforts begun years before by Sallie Renau and continued by Annie Peyton paid off as the state legislature established the Industrial Institute and College for the education of girls "in the arts and sciences." The trustees of the Columbus Female Institute took an active role in the legislative efforts. The legislature had been considering a bill that would establish a state female college in February 1884, and on February 15 the trustees began taking the steps necessary to enable the campus to be donated the state.

The trustees' plan called for the stockholders of the school to sell it to persons who would then donate the school and campus to the state. On March 15, the trustees sent a committee to Jackson with authority to do what was needed to secure Columbus as the location of the state female college. On June 19, 1884, after the trustees had published notice of a public sale, James Sykes, Charles Locke and James Bell bought the Columbus Female Institute. They paid $100 for the school property so that it could then be legally donated to the state.

The Columbus offer was accepted, and the state then added a clock tower to the belfry on "Old Main" (now Callaway Hall) and built the Orr Building next door. In addition, Moore Hall (where Whitfield Hall is now located) and the other buildings of the former Columbus Female Institute were reused. In October 1885, the Industrial Institute and College opened its first session at what had been the Columbus Female Institute.

The establishment of a state female college made national news and was the subject of an illustrated article in *Frank Leslie's Illustrated Newspaper* of New York on July 4, 1885. The paper reported that the grounds and buildings acquired for the college "will be one of, if not the most capacious and imposing buildings for the purpose in the country." The account concluded by stating, "In this Institute and College, Mississippi has set an example which we hope to see followed by other States, until our girls everywhere can gain such an education as will fit them for the practical and profitable employments of life."

Some Things Don't Change

This fall I have again heard the tales of woe from parents of college students. It seems that once again many young people are, as Doonesbury once put it, attending a fraternity or sorority assuming that it is bound to be affiliated with some college. No matter how times change, they really do often stay the same.

The propensity for young people to have a good time at college is nothing new. I thoroughly enjoyed my six and a half years in Oxford, where I got a BA and a juris doctor. I recall in the old records of the DKE fraternity, of which I was a member at Ole Miss, references to members once bringing their shotguns and bird dogs to campus and their dorm rooms for the fall semester.

One former fraternity member, William B. Lowry (a one-time Noxubee County resident), was captain of the University Greys, the campus military unit prior to and during the Civil War. Lowry seemed to have had a most enjoyable time as a student, especially when he discovered that as captain of the university's military unit he could be neither expelled nor suspended from school for rowdy behavior or failing to attend class.

A taste of college life at the turn of the century was found in a 1908–1909 Ole Miss student handbook. Within its pages a student had apparently practiced writing poetry for his English class. One of his poems reflected his not-so-happy view of springtime:

> *The most melancholy days have come,*
> *the saddest of the year.*
> *A little too hot for whiskey,*
> *a little too cold for beer.*

My grandfather, T.C. Billups, also attended Ole Miss and had been in the DKE fraternity. He was there from 1908 to 1912. His brother, James S. Billups, was another DKE. He graduated in 1902 with a degree in pharmacy but returned to Columbus to farm. They both had a most enjoyable college experience, and one of their stories is the perfect example of every event having two sides—each being a matter of perspective.

It all began with a sixtieth anniversary party for the DKE chapter at Ole Miss in April 1910. There was a grand "German Banquet" with "a large attendance of members from many points in this state." Although the banquet was in Oxford, there was at least one side trip.

T.C. Billups and James S. Billups of Columbus at a Delta Kappa Epsilon fraternity party in Oxford. Taken around the time of an April 1910 "road trip" to Senatobia, Mississippi. *Courtesy of Billups-Garth Archives, Columbus-Lowndes Public Library.*

The story of that "road trip" is found in clippings from two different pages of what was apparently an April 1910 Senatobia newspaper. One account appeared on the society page. It stated, "Winston Smith, Roger Montgomery, Cham Conner and T.C. Billups, students at Oxford," had been visiting in Senatobia. The article went on to say that "the young gentlemen came in Automobiles and during their stay had many enjoyable rides with young ladies and friends."

It sounded like a most pleasant and relaxing visit, until you see the headlines in the local news: "Citizens Call Upon Mayor to Take Action Upon Automobiles." The article told how "Senatobia does not boast of any automobile of its own but during the past few days there have been quite a number of visiting ones which have caused considerable commotion among the horses and incidentally among those who drive them."

The report continued to say how some of the "leading citizens in town called upon the Mayor Monday afternoon requesting that the Board of

Mayor and Alderman take some action looking to the protection of the citizens of the town from accidents caused by the unrestrictive use of Automobiles in the town. It was desired that a law be passed prohibiting the use of automobiles on the streets of the town."

How people view something has an awful lot to do with which side of the fence they are standing on or, in this case, riding on. And I guess college students really haven't changed much either.

THE MYSTERY OF "MA"

The 1890s Friendship Cemetery square of Thomas Carleton Billups II often draws attention because of its large angel statue. It is an angel that faces west rather than the traditional east. What few people notice is a small Celtic cross headstone that reads simply "Ma" and underneath "Rest In Peace."

In 1889, Carleton Billups and his wife, Ida Sykes, built a large three-story Eastlake-style home at 905 Main Street in Columbus. The enjoyment of their new home was short-lived, as three years later Ida Sykes Billups became ill and died. Carleton was left to raise two teenage daughters and two young sons.

Knowing that he needed help, he hired a governess to help raise the children. Here the mystery begins. Carleton hired a lady known as "Ma" to be the governess. No one in the family knew who she was or where she came from. All that was known was that her name was Margaret Godson and she was a very devout Catholic. The Billupses were active members of First Methodist Church.

Ma became more than just a governess; she became a member of the family. She was loved by the children, but her background was never told to them. She was simply called Ma. Though the Billupses had many photographs taken in the 1890s and early 1900s, there is only one that shows Ma. The faded circa 1900 photo shows a little old lady in a very plain dress standing in the backyard of the Billups home.

Carleton died in 1898, and Ma, with the help of the older daughters, continued to raise the young boys. Still, no one seemed to know who she was or where she came from. She had become such a part of the family that the children accepted her mysterious past without question.

Ma died in 1903 and was buried on the Billups square in Friendship Cemetery. She left her few possessions to the Billups children. One of her

Oil painting titled *Bride of Heaven* and signed by F.A. Luckett of Columbus, Mississippi. It was a prized possession of Ma's.

prized possessions was an oil painting of a nun titled *Bride of Heaven*. It was signed "F.A. Luckett, Columbus, Mississippi." She left the painting to T.C. Billups III, the youngest child.

Billups family tradition still maintains that nothing was ever known about who Ma was or where she came from. The stories only mention the loving care she gave the children and her being considered a member of the family—one whose past was never mentioned.

When told of the story, Bob Raymond decided to do some digging. What he found was that Margaret Godson was born in Ireland in 1830 and immigrated to the United States in 1852. However, her life story from 1830 to 1852 remains a mystery. To the Billups children her past was of no concern, and they only cared to remember her as Ma. Several months after this column ran in the paper I received an email from a member of the Godson family in Great Britain stating that Margaret was an ancestor who had left for America in the mid-1800s and was never heard from again.

The Legend of Black Creek

In 1851, Joseph B. Cobb published a book titled *Mississippi Scenes*. It contained one of northeast Mississippi's earliest ghost stories, "The Legend of Black Creek." Four miles north of Columbus and just north of the Highway 12 railroad overpass, Andrew Jackson's Military Road crosses a meandering stream known as Black Creek. The old road has been straightened, and the area is now residential—but it once was not so.

Cobb described the Black Creek crossing as "a forbidding spot, shaded by huge willows and swamp oaks, whose thick foliage imparts an aspect of gloom and terror sufficiently ominous to put a suspicious soul on his guard, independent even of the ghostly associations connected with its history."

Black Creek was associated with several "awful deeds." A young Indian "had slain his brother in a fit of anger, and then thrown his body, tied to a large bundle of stones...[into] a sudden sink in the channel of the creek." It was the scene of a horrible ambush, robbery and murder. The melancholy crossing was also well known as the place where several people had drowned attempting to cross Black Creek when it was flooded.

The most noted tragic incident, though, occurred around 1817. Cobb related the story:

> *An aged Tennessean, who died in the county many years ago, and who had been a soldier in the Army of General Jackson, often told the story of how Old Hickory, having arrived on the banks during a tremendous freshet, and being impatient to get along, rashly ordered two young dragoons to try the depth of the ford, and how both of them were swept away by the swift current, and never seen more.*
>
> *Those two soldiers were said to haunt the Military Road crossing, making their appearance on dark moonless or cloudy nights. It was told that at such times one could behold; "two men on horseback with plumes in their caps, and great crooked swords dangling at their sides, rearing and plunging through the air about the height that the creek usually rises*

Black Creek is said to be haunted by "men on horseback with plumes in their caps, and great crooked swords."

to in a high flood, whilst a great white figure [darts] *up suddenly with a shriek out of the dark pool, and then* [falls] *back heavily again, as if pulled with a dead weight.*

So goes the 1851 ghost story of the "Legend of Black Creek." Is there a historical basis? Andrew Jackson ordered the construction of the Military Road but never traveled this segment. However, not far north of Black Creek, on a hill over looking Howard Creek, is a circa 1817 grave of a U.S. soldier who died during the construction of Military Road.

Was It the Ghost of Norman Staples?

The first steamboats on the upper Tombigbee River appeared around 1822. Over the next one hundred years many boats sank, burned or exploded, but only two disasters have left well-known ghost stories.

The burning of the steamboat *Eliza Battle* in 1858, on a freezing, flooded Tombigbee during a winter storm, is the most famous of the ghost stories. That story is based on the absolute horror of the boat's loss, but it does not compare in strange and supernatural associations with the 1913 loss of the steamer *James T. Staples*.

I first encountered the *James T. Staples* in Kathryn Tucker Windham's 1982 book, *Jeffery's Latest 13: More Alabama Ghosts*. However, it was when I read the January 13, 1913 *Columbus Commercial* that I realized how strange the steamer's story really was.

Norman Staples was one of the most successful Mobile steamboat owners around 1900. He owned two very profitable boats and, in 1908, decided to build the most palatial boat built on the Tombigbee since the Civil War and the golden age of steamboats. It was a large, luxurious boat—easily recognized by a huge star hung between its smokestacks. He named the boat the *James T. Staples* after his father.

However, there was one thing that Norman Staples had not counted on. The year 1912 saw all-weather roads beginning to be built throughout the Tombigbee Valley, and motor vehicles started transporting goods. The day of the steamboat had ended.

By late 1912, Norman Staples's boats were losing money, and he was having severe financial problems. The *James T. Staples* was Norman's pride and joy, but he lost it to creditors in December 1912. Staples could not accept the loss of his steamboat and in early January 1913 took his own life with a shotgun.

Shortly after Staples's funeral, the new owners of the steamer *James T. Staples* wanted it to run its regular route up the Tombigbee. The captain responded that it was disrespectful to sail so soon after the funeral and quit. Many of the crew members also quit, reporting that they had seen Norman Staples's ghost wandering the steamboat. As the new crew boarded the steamer, rats and mice were seen jumping off the boat.

Finally, the boat pulled away from the Mobile wharf and headed upriver. It stopped in Coffeeville, Alabama, for cargo. On the landing there was found an old man who had spent his life on the river. For good luck, boat

The steamer *James T. Staples* at the Demopolis, Alabama, landing around 1911.

crews always asked him if they would have a profitable trip. This time his response was that the boat would never return.

Norman Staples had just been buried at Bladon Springs Cemetery, which was located near the river and up stream from Coffeeville. When the *James T. Staples* reached the place on the river closest to its former owner's grave its boilers exploded, killing twenty-six people and sinking the boat.

Survivors were rescued by local citizens and placed on the steamer *John Quill* to be carried to Mobile. The *John Quill* was a steamboat that, in 1912, ran from Columbus to Mobile. The January 13, 1913 *Columbus Commercial* had a front-page account of the loss of the *James T. Staples* and actually commented on the strange circumstance surrounding the disaster.

REFLECTIONS OF A THIRTEENTH-CENTURY GEM

Often within our communities we find an architecturally and historically important building that we are so used to seeing we take it for granted. Here in Columbus, the Church of the Annunciation is such a structure.

The church is a Mississippi Landmark and a great example of a type of Gothic form rarely found in the South. In her book *Historic Architecture in Mississippi*, Mary Wallace Crocker called Annunciation Church "an architectural gem." Not only a part of the historic fabric of Columbus, it is also one of the most architecturally significant religious structures in Mississippi.

Although Annunciation's construction did not begin until 1863, its inspiration and appearance go back 764 years to the gothic chapel of Sainte-Chapelle in Paris. La Sainte-Chapelle, which means "The Holy Chapel," was commissioned by King Louis IX of France. It was built to hold Louis's collection of holy relics, which was said to have included Christ's "Crown of Thorns." Construction began around 1239, and the chapel was completed in 1248. The Paris chapel underwent extensive restoration from 1837 to 1857 and in 1862 was declared a French National Historic Monument.

Columbus did not have a large Catholic population prior to the Civil War, and a Catholic church had never been constructed. All of that changed with the outbreak of war and Columbus becoming a Confederate manufacturing, supply and hospital center. In his 1909 book, *A History of Columbus, Mississippi, During the 19th Century*, Dr. W.L. Lipscomb wrote that "Columbus was almost doubled in white population and the number of Catholics increased to such an extent that they were enabled to build the present Catholic church for their worship."

In response to the rapidly increasing Catholic population, not only in Columbus but throughout northeast Mississippi, the Catholic Church sent Father Jean Baptist Mouton to minister to the needs of the growing population. Father Mouton moved to Columbus and centered his ministry from there. Born in France, Father Mouton was not only a priest but also an

The Church of the Annunciation is an example of a type of Gothic form rarely found in the South. It is patterned after the chapel of Sainte-Chapelle in Paris and is a Mississippi Landmark.

architect. He designed the new church for Columbus. Both the exterior and interior design of the new church reflect scaled-down elements of Sainte-Chapelle. Being a native of France, Father Mouton may have been inspired by the extensive restoration of the Paris chapel, which had occurred only a few years before he designed Annunciation.

The cornerstone of Annunciation Church was laid on May 4, 1863, and construction commenced. One of the problems of wartime construction is that the best materials are not always available for civilian projects. That problem surfaced with the brick used in the church's construction. The bricks that were used turned out to be of inferior quality, and in 1878, the exterior of the church had to be stuccoed.

In a previous section of this book I asked Ken P'Pool, the longtime head of the Mississippi Department of Archives and History's Historic Preservation Division, what he considered to be Columbus's five most interesting buildings.

One of the five was the Church of the Annunciation, which he considered to be the most interesting of all the many historic churches in the town.

Ken described the church in the following way: "the tall, narrow form and the apsidal plan of Sainte-Chapelle are closely duplicated in the Columbus church...The facade of the church is an eclectic assortment of French Gothic motifs. It's three-bay composition is a typically French ploy that dates to the earliest Gothic cathedrals...the interior also imitates features of Sainte-Chapelle." Each of the interior columns and piers is painted to appear to be marble.

In a 1917 article about Columbus in *Collier's Weekly*, Julian Street wrote of the destruction of historic buildings and churches in Columbus: "Columbus may perhaps appreciate the charm of its old homes, but there is evidence to show that it did not appreciate certain other weatherworn structures of great beauty...[The destruction of] these early buildings represents an irreparable loss to Columbus and it is to be hoped that the town will some day be sufficiently enlightened to know this."

The people of Annunciation Church are to be commended, for they appreciate the beauty and value of their old structure and have made plans to restore it. The entire community needs to come together and help support the restoration of this important Mississippi Landmark.

The Boy Scouts and the Little Sister of Liberty

Last week I was talking with David Trojan, and he asked me if I knew the story behind the Statue of Liberty on Main Street in Columbus. I knew it had been given by Irvine Weitzenhoffer and T.M. McGahey, but I did not know the full story. David had become interested in the statue and had explored its history.

He found that the statue's history was as clear as the "other" plaque on the statue or a visit to the web page of the Pushmataha Area Council of the Boy Scouts. Like other buildings and objects I pass by every day, I had never taken the time to stop and pay real close attention to it. I always just enjoyed it as a very nice replica, without stopping to read all of the inscriptions on its base. Though Weitzenhoffer (vice-president of Seminole Manufacturing) and T.M. McGahey (Columbus Marble Works) had erected the miniature

A project of the Boy Scouts of America in 1950, the Columbus Main Street Statue of Liberty was one of two hundred "Little Sisters of Liberty" placed around the United States.

Statue of Liberty, it was actually part of a 1950 national Boy Scout project called the "Crusade to Strengthen the Arm of Liberty." The story that David found gives increased meaning to Columbus's "Little Sister of Liberty."

The project was in celebration of scouting's fortieth anniversary and was meant to be a visible "pledge of everlasting fidelity and loyalty" to America. The project originated with J.P. Whitaker, a Kansas City scout leader and businessman. Approximately two hundred of the eight-foot-high statues, which cost about $350 each and weigh 290 pounds, were placed in cities and towns in thirty-nine states and several territories. They were made from thin copper plates mounted on wooden frames by Friedley-Voshardt Co. of Chicago. The statues were referred to as "Little Sisters of Liberty."

In Columbus, the Pushmataha Area Council was and still is the local Boy Scout organization. It was under its auspices that one of the "Little Sisters of Liberty" was purchased and placed in Columbus on a polished granite base at the intersection of Seventh and Main Streets.

The statue was dedicated on the afternoon of December 7, 1950. An account of the dedication ceremony was in the following day's *Commercial Dispatch*. The paper described the weather as bitter cold, but the dedication was still attended by a "crowd" of scouts. The statue was unveiled by Eagle Scout Fraser Triplett of Louisville. He then formally presented it to Columbus mayor William Hairston, who accepted it on behalf of the citizens of Columbus.

A dedication address was given by Columbus attorney Roger Landrum. In his address he recalled that it was the ninth anniversary of the attack on Pearl Harbor. He then spoke of the troubled times that the Cold War had brought. The crowd was said to be shivering in the cold as Landrum addressed them and said, "There is a bewilderment among the American people today as they face seemingly insurmountable problems without intelligent national leadership."

He concluded his speech by saying that if the American people would rely on initiative and resources and trust in God, "neither the nation nor the Statue of Liberty would crumble."

Of the original two hundred "Little Sisters of Liberty" that were placed around the United States by scouts some sixty-one years ago, the Columbus statue is one of about one hundred that have survived.

Sources

In writing my weekly columns, I found that in answering questions from the public or delving into local history topics, traditional methods of scholarly research often did not work. When writing about individuals of the not-so-distant past, my primary source was frequently relatives or friends who recalled stories and family traditions. I also depended on period newspaper accounts of both recent events and events from the distant past. With both newspapers and oral traditions, I found that the stories were not always the most accurate accounts but best provided the sense or flavor of the times.

Niles' Weekly Register was a wonderful source of information for the early 1800s, as were *Harper's Weekly* and *Frank Leslie's Illustrated Newspaper* for the mid-1800s. As a columnist for the *Commercial Dispatch*, I had access to the newspaper's morgue, which contained papers dating back to the early 1900s. The *Dispatch* may also be found on microfilm at the Columbus-Lowndes Public Library and most area university libraries. I made extensive use of the Billups-Garth Archives, which contain local government and court records dating back to 1821, as well as extensive manuscript collections and vertical files. Its collection amounts to over 1,000 cubic feet, and I think I have visited about 998 of those feet.

When all else failed to answer a question, I called on friends who are always ready to help. Each has areas of expertise in history, genealogy or natural history. Their combined input provided multidisciplinary answers to many questions, and their assistance deserves more than just an acknowledgement.

Below is a list of significant sources and recommended readings:

Botkin, B.A. *A Treasury of Southern Folklore*. New York: Bonanza Books, 1980.

Coates, Robert M. *The Outlaw Years*. New York: The Maculay Company, 1930.

Doster, James, and David C. Weaver. *Tenn-Tom Country: The Upper Tombigbee Valley*. Tuscaloosa: University of Alabama Press, 1997.

Edge, John T. *A Gracious Plenty*. New York: G.P. Putnam's Sons, 1999.

Elliott, Jack D. Jr. "The Plymouth Fort and the Creek War: A Mystery Solved." *The Journal of Mississippi History* 62:4 (2000).

Elliott, Jack D. Jr., and Mary Ann Wells. *Cotton Gin Port: A Frontier Settlement on the Upper Tombigbee*. Jackson: Mississippi Historical Society, 2003.

Gaines, Colonel George S. "Reminiscences of Early Times in the Mississippi Territory." *Mobile Register*, June–July 1872. Reprinted in Kaye, et al, *By the Flow of the Inland River: The Settlement of Columbus, Mississippi, to 1825*.

Gibbs, W. E. "Columbus in Its Growth and Infancy." *Columbus Index*, 1872.

Hamilton, Peter J. *Colonial Mobile*. Tuscaloosa: University of Alabama Press, 1976.

Hudson, Charles. *Knights of Spain, Warriors of the Sun*. Athens: University of Georgia Press, 1997.

Kaye, Samuel H., Rufus Ward and Carolyn B. Neault. *By the Flow of the Inland River: The Settlement of Columbus, Mississippi, to 1825*. Columbus, MS: Snapping Turtle Press, 1992.

Kilby, Clyde S. *Tolkien & The Silmarillion*. Wheaton, IL: Harold Shaw Publishers, 1976.

Kurlansky, Mark. *The Food of a Younger Land*. New York: Riverhead Books, 2009.

Lincecum, Gideon. *Autobiography of Gideon Lincecum*. Publications of the Mississippi Historical Society. No. 8 (1905).

Lincecum, Jerry Bryan, and Edward Hake Phillips. *Adventures of a Frontier Naturalist: The Life and Times of Gideon Lincecum.* College Station: Texas A&M University Press, 1994.

Lipscomb, Dr. W.L. *A History of Columbus, Mississippi During the 19th Century.* Birmingham, AL: Press of Dispatch Printing Co., 1909.

Lisowski, Connie L., and Kenneth D. Lusignan. "A History of Columbus Air Force Base." Columbus Air Force Base: Office of History, 2008.

Lord, Walter. *A Night to Remember.* New York: Henry Holt and Company, 1955.

Matthiessen, Peter. *Wildlife in America.* New York: Viking, 1987.

Neville, Bert. *Directory of River Packets in the Mobile-Alabama-Warrior-Tombigbee Trades, 1818–1932.* Alabama, 1962.

Pate, James P., ed., *The Reminiscences of George Strother Gaines.* Tuscaloosa: University of Alabama Press, 1998.

Romans, Bernard. *A Concise Natural History of East and West Florida.* 1775. Reprint, New Orleans: Pelican Publishing Company, 1961.

Segrest, James, and Mark Hoffman. *Moanin' at Midnight: The Life and Times of Howlin' Wolf.* New York: Thunder's Mouth Press, 2004.

Sherman, Harry L., ed. "A Very Remarkable Bluff." MUW Plymouth Bluff Center, 2007.

Vaughn, Estelle Rogers. *Southern-Born and Bred.* Chicago: Adams Press, 1972.

Ward, Rufus. "A Guide to the Use of 19th Century Court Records in the Billups-Garth Archives of the Columbus-Lowndes Public Library." Digital manuscript, Billups-Garth Archives of the Columbus-Lowndes Public Library, 2008.

———. *The Tombigbee River Steamboats: Rollodores, Dead Heads and Side-Wheelers.* Charleston, SC: The History Press, 2010.

About the Author

R ufus Ward has been active in the fields of history and historic preservation for more than thirty-five years. He divides his time between consulting and lecturing on cultural projects and writing a weekly history column for the *Commercial Dispatch* in Columbus, Mississippi. He also serves as an instructor for Mississippi University for Women's Life Enrichment Program. Ward is the author of The History Press's *The Tombigbee River Steamboats: Rollodores, Dead Heads and Side-Wheelers* and has been a contributing author for two other books—*After Removal: The Choctaw in Mississippi* and *By the Flow of the Inland River: The Settlement of Columbus, Mississippi, to 1825*. He resides in West Point, Mississippi, with his wife, Karen, and bird dog, Eliza Faye.

Visit us at
www.historypress.net